CULTURES OF THE WORLD
Wales

Anna Hestler and Jo-Ann Spilling

mc **Marshall Cavendish**
Benchmark
New York

PICTURE CREDITS
Cover: © keith morris /Alamy
Audrius Tomonis: 138 • Corbis: 29, 34, 35, 38, 41, 42, 45, 49, 52, 67, 71, 98, 101, 102, 105, 119 • Getty Images: 5, 43, 47, 48, 55, 64, 69, 74, 118 • Hulton Getty Picture Library: 26, 27, 28 • International Photobank: 23, 84 • John R. Jones: 9, 17, 77, 80, 103, 117 • North Wind Pictures Archives: 20, 21, 22, 24, 25 • Photolibrary: 1, 3, 6, 7, 8, 10, 11, 12, 13, 14, 15, 16, 18, 19, 30, 33, 36, 37, 39, 40, 44, 46, 50, 51, 53, 54, 56, 57, 58, 59, 60, 61, 62, 65, 66, 68, 70, 72, 73, 75, 76, 78, 79, 81, 82, 83, 85, 86, 87, 88, 89, 90, 91, 92, 93, 94, 95, 96, 97, 99, 100, 104, 106, 107, 108, 109, 110, 111, 114, 115, 116, 120, 121, 122, 123, 124, 125, 126, 127, 128, 129, 130, 131 • Trip Photographic Library: 31, 32, 63, 112, 113

PRECEDING PAGE
Reflections of the rugged mountains bounce off the Pentwyn Reservoir at the Brecon Beacons National Park in Powys.

Publisher (U.S.): Michelle Bisson
Editors: Deborah Grahame-Smith, Mindy Pang
Copyreader: Sherry Chiger
Designers: Nancy Sabato, Benson Tan
Cover picture researcher: Tracey Engel
Picture researcher: Joshua Ang

Marshall Cavendish Benchmark
99 White Plains Road
Tarrytown, NY 10591
Website: www.marshallcavendish.us

© Times Media Private Limited 2001
© Marshall Cavendish International (Asia) Private Limited 2011
® "Cultures of the World" is a registered trademark of Times Publishing Limited.

Originated and designed by Times Media Private Limited
An imprint of Marshall Cavendish International (Asia) Private Limited
A member of Times Publishing Limited

Marshall Cavendish is a trademark of Times Publishing Limited.

All Internet sites were correct and accurate at the time of printing. All monetary figures in this publication are in U.S. dollars.

Library of Congress Cataloging-in-Publication Data
Hestler, Anna.
  Wales / Anna Hestler and Jo-Ann Spilling. — 2nd ed.
    p. cm. — (Cultures of the world)
  Includes bibliographical references and index.
  Summary: "Provides comprehensive information on the geography, history,
    wildlife, governmental structure, economy, cultural diversity, peoples,
    religion, and culture of Wales"--Provided by publisher.
  ISBN 978-1-60870-457-6
  1. Wales—Juvenile literature. I. Spilling, Jo-Ann. II. Title.
  DA708.H47 2011
  942.9—dc22   2010030339

Printed in China
7 6 5 4 3 2 1

CONTENTS

INTRODUCTION

WALES, TOGETHER WITH ENGLAND, SCOTLAND, AND NORTHERN Ireland, is part of the United Kingdom. But although Wales is directly west of England, it has a distinct culture, rooted in Celtic history, along with its own language and a strong musical and cultural tradition. It is famous for its choirs, and many Welsh people enjoy their national sport of rugby. The leek is the national emblem of Wales, and daffodils are often used as a symbol of the country. The Welsh name for their own country is *Cymru* (COME-ree), which means "fellow countrymen." The Anglo-Saxons called the country Wales, meaning "stranger," because the Celts living there spoke a foreign language and lived differently from them. Although English has become the main language, more and more Welsh people are learning and reclaiming their own language. The country is blessed with breathtaking scenery, including many spectacular mountains, hills, valleys, rivers, and historical castles. To many visitors, Wales is known as a land with a warm and welcoming spirit. As the Welsh would say in their own language, *Croeso i Gymru* (KROY-so-e-GUM-ree)—Welcome to Wales.

GEOGRAPHY

Reflections of Mount Snowdon, the highest mountain in Wales, in Llyn Llydaw in Snowdonia National Park.

CHAPTER 1

WALES HAS A TOTAL LAND AREA OF 8,108 square miles (21,000 square km) and is about half of the size of Massachusetts in the United States. It is part of Great Britain, which also consists of England and Scotland, and is surrounded by the Irish Sea on the north, Saint George's Channel and Cardigan Bay on the west, and the Bristol Channel on the south. The only land border is on the east with England.

Wales is a small but beautiful country surrounded mainly by water. The landscape of Wales is remarkably diverse, and the weather is much like that of the rest of Great Britain—cool summers, cold winters, and lots of rain!

A view over the village of Treorchy and the Rhondda Valley from Bwlch Y Clawdd.

NORTH WALES

Colorful seashores, big beaches, green hills, and rugged peaks—north Wales has it all. The highest mountains are found in Snowdonia National Park, named after Mount Snowdon, the highest mountain in England and Wales, standing at 3,560 feet (1,085 m). This was the training ground for the first successful expedition to climb Mount Everest.

Farther south, the peak of Cadair Idris looms into view. To the northeast, rising above the lush Vale of Clwyd are the smooth Clwydian Hills, a natural barrier between England and Wales. Off the northwest coast, the Isle of Anglesey is separated from the mainland by the Menai Strait but is joined by two bridges. Just below Anglesey, the Lleyn Peninsula juts into the Irish Sea.

The snow-covered mountain of Cadair Idris leaves many spellbound.

MID-WALES

Mid-Wales runs from the River Dyfi to the mouth of the River Teifi and east to the border with England. It contains part of Snowdonia National Park and a sliver of the Brecon Beacons. Mid-Wales is an area of tranquil beauty—a blend of green fields, gentle hills, majestic mountains, and sweeping shores.

The ancient and austere slopes of the Cambrian Mountains are frequented by climbers and trekkers. Those who prefer the sea head west to the coast along Cardigan Bay, an area with beaches and charming towns such as Aberystwyth, a lively university town. Farther down the coast, the town of New Quay has a wildlife hospital for seabirds and marine creatures. Inland, there are remote lakes, waterfalls, and cool forests that offer wonderful woodland walks.

SOUTH AND WEST WALES

This region extends from the leafy Wye Valley on the border with England to the western tip of Pembrokeshire. This spectacular area is full of unexpected contrasts, including two very different national parks: Pembrokeshire Coast

Handsome, colorful Georgian houses overlook the harbor of Tenby, one of Wales's premier resorts.

Both Skomer and Skokholm islands have colonies of guillemots, razorbills, storm petrels, kittiwakes, and puffins.

A waterfall brims over the jagged rocks at Brecon Beacons National Park in Powys.

and Brecon Beacons. The Pembrokeshire Coast National Park is Britain's only coastal park and is full of rare wildlife and spectacular flowers. The Welsh national flower, the yellow daffodil, grows freely in the charming seaside town of Tenby. The gentle Preseli Hills, not too far away, are shrouded in mystery because the stones that make up the inner circle of Stonehenge were quarried here. Nobody is quite sure how they were transported to England.

Inland, Brecon Beacons National Park is gorgeous, with wide-open spaces and grassy summits. When English novelist Daniel Defoe came to visit in the 17th century, he said, "The English call it Breakneckshire, 'tis mountainous to the extremity." The classic walk in the park is to the top of Pen y Fan, the highest point in southern Wales at 2,907 feet (886 m). Although the southern mountains look enticing, they can be quite foreboding when brisk winds combine with heavy mists and rain. It is no wonder the Brecon Beacons are used as a training ground for the army.

The southern coast is more industrialized, but there are still fine stretches of natural beauty, such as the breezy Gower Peninsula and the Glamorgan Heritage Coast, which has some mountainous dunes that contain medieval villages that gradually became covered in sand. Much of the beauty of the valleys in southern Wales was scarred by the coal industry, but the area is now returning to its past splendor, thanks to the government's land-reclamation program.

RIVERS AND LAKES

Wales has many rivers, streams, and lakes, and some offer excellent fishing opportunities. The longest rivers are the Dee, Severn, and Wye, which flow through the lowlands along the English border. The Severn, which empties into the Bristol Channel, is one of the longest rivers in England and Wales. The Wye is a great salmon river, and the surrounding area was a source of inspiration for the poet William Wordsworth.

There are many lovely lakes, including Bala Lake (also known as Llyn Tegid) in northern Wales. This is the largest natural lake in Wales. It is a popular spot for water sports and home to a unique fish called a gwyniad, which is related to the salmon. Llangorse Lake is the largest natural lake in southern Wales. According to legend, this lake covers an ancient city. It is known for certain that lake dwellers used to live on an artificial island that can still be seen from the shore.

The serene Bala Lake in Snowdonia National Park.

Conifer forests can still be found in Tregaron, Wales.

Wales also has a number of artificial lakes, waterways, and reservoirs. Llyn Brianne, a reservoir that serves the southwest, was built with the protection of the natural environment in mind. A special fish trap was constructed below its dam to trap salmon swimming upstream to spawn. The salmon are then collected and driven beyond the dam in a van equipped with a special breathing tank. The Monmouthshire and Brecon Canal, built in 1812, was used for the transportation of raw materials between Brecon and Newport and is now popular with leisure boaters.

FLORA

About 5,000 years ago, Wales was covered in oak forests. Although pockets of woodland remain, most of the forests have disappeared due to forest clearance and overgrazing, which has prevented regrowth. Much of Wales is now covered by induced grassland and plantation woodland and dominated by conifers, which provide timber but not a welcoming habitat for birds and other animals. Pengelli Forest in Pembrokeshire, home to both English midland hawthorn and oak trees, is most representative of the ancient Welsh forests.

Wales has many beautiful wild plants and flowers. Vivid violet sea lavender and white water lilies can be found around the freshwater lakes. The coastal sand dunes support marram grass, sea holly, and evening primroses. Delicate purple saxifrages decorate the slopes of the Brecon Beacons. The white Snowdon lily carpets the slopes of Mount Snowdon, but it can be seen only in late May and early June.

Many of the islands off southern Wales are official nature reserves. Because of their exposure to harsh winds, the vegetation is largely shrubby heath and herb-rich grassland. The largest and most accessible island is Skomer Island, which has colorful rock gardens with red campion. To its south lies Skokholm Island, where purple-red rocks are smothered with spongy lichen. Apart from these islands, there are five Areas of Outstanding Natural Beauty in Wales; the Gower Peninsula, the Lleyn Peninsula, the Isle of Anglesey, the Clwydian Range, and the Wye Valley.

The beautiful coastal landscape of Skokholm Island in Wales.

A group of puffins standing on the edge of a cliff in coastal Wales.

FAUNA

The Welsh coastline has some of the best seabird breeding colonies in Europe. One of the world's largest gannet colonies is on Grassholm Island, with 39,292 pairs of these magnificent white birds. Ramsey Island is home to a rare chough, and more than 50 percent of the Manx shearwater population lives on Bardsey Island. Bardsey Island used to be a place of pilgrimage and is said to be the burial place of 20,000 holy men.

Inland, the hills and the valleys are alive with birdsong. Mid-Wales is home to the red kite. These graceful, reddish birds of prey nearly became extinct in the 1930s. Since then, a great deal of effort has been made to protect them, but there are still only about 200 breeding pairs in mid-Wales. One of the United Kingdom's most endangered birds, the hen harrier, also lives in the hills of Wales.

Wales is home to a range of mammals as well. The pine marten, which resembles a cat, lives in the wooded mountains and hills, and black-eyed polecats are found around Snowdonia and along the coastal dunes. The Welsh pony is a familiar sight in the foothills, as are wild goats on the harsh mountain slopes. Skomer Island has a special island species of vole, and along the rocky coast, ringed seals bask in the sunshine.

CITIES AND TOWNS

Cardiff is the capital city of Wales. One is more likely to hear English than Welsh spoken here, and the population is one of the most cosmopolitan in Wales.

The history of Cardiff goes back to the Romans, who built forts along the River Taff around A.D. 55. At the beginning of the 19th century, Cardiff was no more than a small town. It grew to become the world's busiest coal-exporting port by 1913, due to its proximity to the southern coal and iron mines. At the height of the coal boom, dozens of ships were anchored just outside the port waiting their turn to enter. But the coal trade began to decline after World War I, and today the docks are closed. The city is now dedicated to commerce and administration. The Cardiff Bay Redevelopment Corporation has successfully redeveloped the entire waterfront to include the architecturally impressive Wales Millennium Centre, the National Assembly Building, and the Millennium Stadium.

A night scene of Cardiff Bay.

Swansea, Wales's maritime city, is justly proud of its 600-berth marina.

Cardiff Castle sits in the heart of the city. Originally a Roman fort, it was later enlarged by the Normans, then renovated in 1872 by William Burges, with the fortune of the third Marquess of Bute. Cardiff also has an elegant Edwardian civic center, built in 1904. The civic buildings are of white Portland cement and include the City Hall, the Law Courts, the National Museum of Wales, and the Temple of Peace and Health.

Swansea is the second-largest city in Wales. The poet Dylan Thomas, who was born here, described it as "an ugly, lovely town." It does have a lovely location on the bay, but it used to be the center of the copper industry and became terribly polluted. Much of the city center was bombed during World War II but has since been rebuilt.

Today the city is a much nicer place to live. It has a modern shopping center, the oldest museum in Wales, and the remains of an old castle. The Guildhall contains the city's main concert hall and an impressive display of murals by

Sir Frank Brangwyn, a Welsh artist. A lot of attention has been directed to the waterfront. The old docklands have been rejuvenated, and there is a huge marina and a Maritime and Industrial Museum with a working woolen mill. A footpath runs along the bay to Mumbles, a quaint seaside resort.

Aberystwyth is located on the beautiful Cardigan Bay and is considered the capital of mid-Wales. It is a university town, a seaside resort, and the headquarters of the Welsh Language Society. The university campus contains an arts center and the National Library of Wales. This library has some of the oldest surviving books and manuscripts in Wales, such as the Black Book of Carmarthen, the oldest book written in Welsh.

Constitution Hill, a steep outcrop on the northern end of the town, can be reached by riding the electric Cliff Railway, built in 1896. Its summit boasts a view of the whole town, from which can be seen the remains of an Iron Age fort and Aberystwyth Castle, built in 1277 by Edward I.

The old University College of Wales, with its mock-Gothic tower, is now the University Theological College. Beyond it lie the pier and promenade, as well as the Cliff Railway on Constitution Hill.

HISTORY

THE HISTORY OF WALES IS CLOSELY tied to that of the rest of the British Isles, and in particular, with its larger and more powerful neighbor, England. Wales has never existed as a separate country but has at times in its history managed to remain independent from the influence of England.

Wales finally lost its independence when it was united with England under the Acts of Union passed during the reign of Henry VIII in 1536 and 1542.

The Saint Brynach's Cross is a pre-Norman Celtic cross.

Throughout the course of their history, the Welsh have struggled against invaders: the Romans, the Saxons, the Vikings, the Normans, and most recently their neighbors, the English.

EARLY INHABITANTS

The earliest inhabitants were hunters and gatherers, and there is little evidence that many settlements or monuments existed before 4000 B.C. At about 4000 B.C., however, Neolithic peoples arrived from the western coasts of Continental Europe to farm the land. They used stone tools and lived in simple houses. They also built great communal graves, both stone tombs concealed under mounds of rubble and long barrows. The stone tombs were probably the burial chambers of important families, some containing elaborately decorated stones, and about 150 of them have been found in Wales. There are also signs that their settlements were attacked and burned in violent local wars.

From about 2300 B.C. onward, people of the Bronze Age arrived from central and northwestern Continental Europe, bringing with them skills in metalwork and more sophisticated bronze tools. They were known as the Beaker People because of the way they buried their dead. They laid out the bodies in stone-lined graves alongside objects such as small clay beakers. It is possible that the beakers contained a special drink associated with the burial ritual.

A Celtic druid carrying mistletoe and a sickle.

THE CELTS

The Celts were an early Indo-European people who developed a distinct culture across much of Europe during the Iron Age, from 700 B.C. In Britain these groups included the Dumnonii in Cornwall, the Dobunni along the upper Thames (modern-day central England), and the Ordovices in Wales. An advanced people, they were weavers, potters, and skilled metalworkers. Their art characteristically used abstract geometric designs and stylized bird and animal forms.

CELTIC WARRIORS

According to contemporary Roman commentators, the Celts were fierce warriors, remarkable for their height, muscularity, and fair coloring. They often painted themselves with blue dye to terrify their opponents in battle. Using a variety of weapons such as iron swords, spears, daggers, and wooden shields, they rode horse-drawn chariots that were fast and agile. During battle, they often hurled javelins and sometimes jumped down from their horses to fight on foot.

No doubt the Romans must have thought twice as they prepared to attack Anglesey, the stronghold of the druids, who were the Celts' religious caste. The Roman historian Tacitus gives a descriptive account of the Celts: "The enemy lined the shores with a dense armed mass. Among them were black-robed women with disheveled hair, like Furies brandishing torches. Close by stood druids, raising their hands to heaven and screaming dreadful curses. At this sight our soldiers were gripped by fear." But the Romans did not retreat. Instead they crossed the strait, slaughtered the druids, and destroyed their holy altars. Despite various rebellions, the Celts were defeated by around 58 B.C. and the druids banned.

Celtic religion was polytheistic, which means they believed in many gods, as well as animist, believing that spirits existed in natural objects such as trees, rivers, and rocks. Especially important were the spirits of springs and lakes. Some of these were thought to possess healing powers, whereas others had the power to grant favors. The modern custom of throwing coins in a fountain for luck may have developed from these Celtic beliefs. The druids were the priestly class in Celtic society, and they were believed to be able to communicate with the gods and have special religious knowledge.

A hand-colored
woodcut of Roman
soldiers in combat.

THE ROMAN CONQUEST

Julius Caesar invaded England around 55 B.C. Despite opposition from Welsh tribes led by Caradog (or Caratacus to the Romans), Roman conquest of England and Wales was completed by A.D. 78. Following the Roman conquest, the various tribes of Celtic-speaking people came to be identified collectively as Britons in Roman histories of the period. These Britons remained in place throughout what is now England as well as Wales and southern Scotland throughout the Roman occupation, and in many respects became quite romanized.

The Romans built military camps and established towns such as Cardiff and Carmarthen. They constructed roads and a great highway called Sarn Helen joining northern and southern Wales. Roman troops traveled up and down this highway, transporting the lead, copper, iron, silver, and gold that they had mined in Wales.

Although the Romans occupied Wales for more than 300 years, they never managed to conquer the whole land. Wales was never fully romanized, and many of its people continued their traditional way of life. By about A.D. 400, increasing pressure from numerous invading tribes and domestic threats forced the Romans to relinquish their control of Britain.

ANGLO-SAXON INVASION

After Roman rule had collapsed, Britain entered the Dark Ages—so named because of the disintegration of Romanic Britain and because only fragments of information survive from this age. Raids by neighbors were commonplace, and by the beginning of the fifth century A.D., Irish tribes had invaded from the west, establishing coastal colonies, and the Picts had invaded from Scotland, in the far north. This period marked the beginning of early Welsh political organization, as Britain became carved up into small warring kingdoms.

An artist's impression of King Arthur's legendary Round Table, hanging on the wall of Winchester Cathedral.

This was also a time of consolidation for Christendom. The Romans had introduced Christianity, but it was spread at this time by traveling saints who converted others to the faith, which is how the Dark Ages in Wales became known as the Age of Saints. One of these saints, Dewi (or David, c. 500—589), became the patron saint of Wales.

Toward the end of the sixth century, Germanic tribes—the Angles, the Saxons, and the Jutes—began crossing the sea from northern Europe and established colonies across eastern and southern England. These tribes advanced steadily throughout Britain and began to push into the Welsh border areas. Their advance was temporarily checked by a great victory, led by a Briton, Ambrosius Aurelianus, over the Anglo-Saxons at a place called Mons Badonicus. Little else is known about this hero, but he lives on in legend as King Arthur. Nevertheless this was a short-lived victory, and the Saxons continued pushing northward and westward. Over the next few hundred

There are different theories about how the great highway Sarn Helen was named. Some say that the name comes from *Sarn y Lleng*, Welsh for "Causeway of the Legions." Others say it means "Helen's Causeway" and was named after Helen, the wife of Magnus Maximus, who was the Roman commander at that time.

years, the weight of the Anglo-Saxon invasion and its steady migration west forced the Britons into the western parts of the British Isles—Wales, Cornwall, and Ireland.

In the eighth century, Offa, the greatest king of the Anglo-Saxon kingdom of Mercia in central England, built a long dike to mark the territory of his kingdom, and the border between England and Wales has been defined by it ever since.

THE 9TH AND 10TH CENTURIES

Throughout the 9th and 10th centuries, Wales was attacked many times by Norse raiders, called Vikings, who came across the North Sea from Scandinavia in longships. Although they established extensive colonies in eastern England, the Vikings never succeeded in colonizing Wales, partly because of the resistance under Rhodri Mawr (Rhodri the Great, c. 820—878) who ruled most of Wales. (His grandson, Hywel Dda, is remembered for introducing a code of law that survived until the arrival of Edward I.) By the latter part of the ninth century, with the help of Welsh kings, Anglo-Saxon king Alfred of Wessex (849—899) had recovered control of much of England from the Danish Vikings.

An artist's impression of a Norse raid.

THE NORMAN CONQUEST

Under the leadership of William the Conqueror, the Normans, who came from France, defeated the Anglo-Saxons in England at the Battle of Hastings in 1066. In order to secure his conquest, William the Conqueror made a pact with Welsh rulers recognizing their authority in their own kingdoms. In the borderlands, called the Marches, Norman lords were given extensive powers as "marcher lords" to keep the local population under control. Meanwhile, from Chester and Shrewsbury, towns on the Welsh-English border, the Normans penetrated farther into Wales. By 1093 the Normans had invaded almost all of southern Wales, including Cardigan, Pembroke, Brecon, and Glamorgan.

The Normans founded market towns throughout Britain, where livestock sales still take place today. They were also great castle builders. Although the Normans managed to colonize the lowlands of southern and mid-Wales, the Welsh language and culture remained strong in the northern highlands. In northern Wales the three Welsh kingdoms of Gwynedd, Powys, and Deheubarth regained power from the Normans by the 12th century.

At about 9 A.M. on October 14, 1066, William I, Duke of Normandy, engaged his 7,000-strong Norman army against a similar-sized English force. William's troops pretended to flee, drawing the English after them. They then turned around and picked the pursuers off one by one, earning William the English crown and the title "the Conqueror."

Literature flourished at this time. *The History of Gryffudd ap Cynan*, by Welsh historian Giraldus Cambrensis (Gerald of Wales), revealed the political and cultural values of Wales during the time of the first king of Gwynedd, Gruffydd ap Cynan. Many epic poems, romances, and legends were recorded for the first time. The oldest book in Welsh is the *Black Book of Carmarthen*, a volume containing the work of court poets and produced around 1250 by Cistercian monks.

By the late 12th century, two great Welsh heroes began the struggle for Welsh independence from the English. The first was Llywelyn ap Iorwerth (Llywelyn the Great), who succeeded in ruling nearly all of north Wales. He sided with the English barons and signed the Magna Carta, obtaining some rights for Wales. This was a short-lived alliance, however; when he died in 1240, the land was divided again.

The battle scene in 1275 during which Llywelyn ap Gruffydd the last Prince of Wales (1224-82), was defeated by English troops.

Later on his grandson Llywelyn ap Gruffydd (Llywelyn the Last) came to power and restored a degree of unity. Proclaiming himself Prince of Wales, he made a treaty in 1267 with the English king, Henry III, to recognize his title, but this peacekeeping measure failed. When Henry died in 1272, Llywelyn refused to accept his successor, Edward I of England, and led a revolt. Edward I invaded Wales in 1277, and Llywelyn was ambushed and killed on December 11, 1282. All hopes of Welsh independence were dashed. In 1284 the Statute of Rhuddlan divided Wales into the Principality (under the direct control of the English royal family) and the Marcher Lordships (under the control of local aristocratic families.

ENGLAND TAKES OVER

After the defeat of Llywelyn the Last, Edward I started a program of castle building, both for security and as a symbol of English power. The mighty Caernarfon Castle, where Edward's son Edward II was born and bestowed with the title Prince of Wales, still towers over the medieval town of Caernarfon. The great Conwy, Harlech, and Beaumaris castles were also built during this time.

Under the rule of Edward I, Wales was administered by the English, with the Welsh in less influential positions of power. The Welsh were discontented with their subordinate position, and eventually a nobleman named Owen Glendower (in Welsh, Owain Glyndŵr) led them in what is known as the Welsh Revolt against the rule of Henry IV of England in 1400. After 14 years the rising was crushed, and Glyndŵr disappeared, his end unknown.

In 1485 Henry Tudor, also known as King Henry VII, ascended the English throne. The Welsh were delighted because the Tudors could trace their ancestry back to Welsh gentry. However, although Henry Tudor gave some Welshmen positions at court, he did not give much attention to Wales as a whole.

Henry Tudor's son Henry VIII legally united Wales with England under the Acts of Union (1536 and 1542). Under these acts, new counties were formed, and Welsh towns were given representation in the English Parliament. For the first time in history, Welshmen enjoyed the same political status as Englishmen.

King Edward I (1272-1307) was a renowned warrior, earning the nickname "Hammer of the Scots."

INDUSTRIAL REVOLUTION AND METHODISM

Henry Tudor's granddaughter Elizabeth became queen of England. She was a tall, striking woman with red hair who governed well and was proud of her Welsh ancestry. To ensure that Protestantism took root in Wales, she allowed an Act of Parliament to be passed that resulted in the New Testament being translated into Welsh in 1567, which in turn helped to keep the Welsh language alive.

The Industrial Revolution changed life throughout Britain in the 18th and 19th centuries. The development of mass manufacturing and heavy industry was a turning point in the history of Wales. New industries sprang up, and many people left rural Wales to work in the coal mines. Large mines were established in south Wales from the 1840s, with many workers laboring under poor working conditions for long hours and low pay. Inevitably this resulted in a great deal of social unrest, including riots.

The Methodist Church revival, which had begun in the 18th century, provided a new source of social unity for Welsh people. The movement focused on Bible study and a methodical approach to understanding Scripture and Christian living. Methodism had its strongest following in the mining valleys of south Wales and the factory towns of the English Midlands. Many of the Welsh who converted to Methodism were motivated by the continued disregard for the ordinary Welsh people by sections of the Welsh gentry and the English Parliament, as well as by the fact that the established church, the Church of England, was pro-English. The Methodist Church established Sunday schools, which became an important feature of Welsh life. Many Welsh people were taught to read and write Welsh in the Sunday schools, which was crucial for the survival of the language, as it was not taught in

Young coal miners at work in the mines at Blaenavon, in north Wales, in 1939.

the government-run schools. The revival of religious feeling through the Methodist Church gave the Welsh a new sense of identity.

The 19th century was a melting pot of movements throughout Britain. Other than religious ideologies, there was also a new sense of political direction in the country. Socialism gained many supporters, mainly in the working-class, industrial towns of south Wales. One of the founders of the British Labour Party, Keir Hardie,

won his parliamentary seat in a Welsh constituency in 1900. In the early part of the 20th century, Wales mainly supported the Liberal Party, particularly when Welshman David Lloyd George became prime minister of the United Kingdom during World War I (1914—18). The Labour Party steadily gained ground, however, and in the years after World War I it replaced the Liberals as the dominant party in Wales.

World War II (1939—45) had a profound effect on Welsh life. After the war, many of the traditional industries, such as coal mining, declined, and the economy went into a slump. By the end of the 20th century, the coal and steel industries in Wales had collapsed, thus causing widespread unemployment and forcing the country to redefine its future.

Welsh desire for home rule grew throughout the 20th century. The Welsh nationalist party, Plaid Cymru (the Party of Wales), was formed in 1925, although it did not win its first parliamentary seat until 1966. Plaid made further gains in elections throughout the 1970s and 1980s, although more Welsh people voted for the Labour Party. However, the newly elected Labour government in 1997 promised votes on establishing local parliaments in both Wales and Scotland. Welsh people narrowly voted in favor of an independent parliament, and a separate Welsh Assembly was set up in 1999. The new Welsh Assembly Building was completed in 2006 and officially opened on March 1, Saint David's Day, that year.

Members of Parliament from Plaid Cymru enter the English Parliament. The Welsh MPs received a particularly warm welcome from their supporters, who waved and sang for their representatives.

GOVERNMENT

The debating chamber in the Senedd of the National Assembly for Wales Building. This modern building uses traditional Welsh materials such as slate and Welsh oak in its construction, and the design is based on the concepts of openness and transparency.

WALES (CYMRU IN WELSH) IS ONE of the countries that make up Great Britain, which also includes England and Scotland. Great Britain and Northern Ireland form the United Kingdom, which is a constitutional monarchy and parliamentary democracy. The four member countries differ from each other in many cultural aspects; thus although there is one government, some aspects of local government are organized differently.

Wales is a part of the United Kingdom of Great Britain and Northern Ireland, with limited independent powers held by the National Assembly for Wales. Those powers not given to the assembly remain with the central government of the United Kingdom, based in London, England.

A Welsh girl wearing traditional costume and carrying a basket of daffodils. The Welsh word for "daffodil" is similar to "leek," which is why both have been adopted as national emblems.

Most countries have ordinary animals for emblems, but Wales has a mythical beast—the dragon. This adorns the green and white background on the national flag. Nobody is quite sure how the red dragon became the emblem of Wales. One theory is that the Romans used the dragon as a military standard, and the Welsh continued this practice after the Romans left. There may be some truth to this because the English word dragon *and the Welsh word* draig *(dryg) are both derived from the Latin root* draco.

The Prince of Wales's feathers are another national emblem of Wales. The crest of ostrich plumes and the German motto, Homout; ich dien *(meaning "Courage; I serve"), were introduced by Edward the Black Prince (1330—76), who became Prince of Wales in 1343. These feathers currently adorn the badge of the national Welsh rugby team.*

THE STRUCTURE OF THE BRITISH GOVERNMENT

Wales is a principality, with a Prince of Wales. It is governed by Whitehall, the United Kingdom's political and administrative center in London, England, and, since 1999, by its own National Assembly in Cardiff. The United Kingdom is unusual in that it does not have a written constitution. Its governing principles are a combination of parliamentary statutes, common law (legal principles based on precedents that can be traced back to Anglo-Saxon times), and convention.

The head of state is Queen Elizabeth II, but in reality, the United Kingdom is governed through the British Parliament in London. Parliament consists of the queen, the House of Lords, and the House of Commons, the latter being the more important of the two houses. The queen appoints the prime minister, who is the leader of the majority party in the House of Commons. All other ministers are appointed based on the advice of the prime minister. The most important ministers make up the cabinet, which works closely with the prime minister to make policy decisions. Wales elects 40 members of Parliament (MPs) to the 646-member House of Commons to participate in the governing of the United Kingdom and look after the interests of their supporters in Wales.

In Parliament, Welsh matters are discussed in the Wales Office (Swyddfa Cymru), which has responsibility for Welsh issues in Westminster, the seat of Parliament. The Wales Office replaced the old Welsh Office, which had extensive control over Welsh politics from its establishment in 1965 until the creation of the National Assembly for Wales in 1999.

The Welsh Assembly debating chamber in the National Assembly for Wales in Cardiff.

The custom of naming the monarch's eldest son the Prince of Wales began in 1301, when King Edward I bestowed this title on his son Prince Edward, who was born at Caernarfon Castle in northwestern Wales. The history of the title goes back to its only Welsh holder, Llywelyn ap Gruffydd, who was recognized as a prince in 1267.

The current Prince of Wales is Prince Charles, eldest son of the current queen, Elizabeth II. Most, but not all, Welsh recognize his title. On the evening before his ceremonial investiture in 1969, two Welsh men blew themselves up while planting explosives at a government office in Abergele, in southwestern Wales. These were the first men to die in the name of Welsh nationalism. Later, at his investiture in Caernarfon Castle, some nationalists wore badges that said, "No English Prince is Prince of Wales."

DEVOLUTION

Various politicians have been pressing for devolution since the 19th century, and the issue has been debated within the ranks of the political parties. In 1956 Megan Lloyd George and S. O. Davies, two Welsh Labour MPs who had been pushing for more independence, presented a petition to Parliament for a Welsh assembly. As a token gesture to appease Welsh nationalists, the ruling Conservative Party appointed a part-time Welsh minister and made the Welsh flag official in 1958.

When the Labour Party won the general election in 1964, it created the post of secretary of state for Wales. Supported by a separate department known as the Welsh Office, this gave Wales a greater say within the UK government. Demands from the Welsh for an elected assembly with powers devolved from Westminster became more strident, which led to an act giving Wales a measure of devolution in 1978. In 1979 the Welsh voted on the issue but rejected the proposal for further devolution. People on both sides of the debate were wary of the consequences. Welsh speakers feared being dominated by the anglicized south, Plaid Cymru (the Welsh nationalist party) was apprehensive that it would lead to Labour Party domination, and there were concerns that devolution would damage an already fragile economy.

In the 1990s the devolution issue was back on the agenda. Devolution proponents argued that it would counter excessive central government control. Their opponents argued that it might encourage conflict with the rest of the United Kingdom. The issue was finally settled by a referendum in 1997 when a slim majority voted in favor of a National Assembly for Wales.

The City Hall in Cardiff, the capital of Wales.

THE NATIONAL ASSEMBLY

Wales is a constituency of the European Parliament in Brussels, Belgium. It currently elects four members of the European Parliament (MEPs).

In 1999 the National Assembly for Wales was created, consisting of a 60-member assembly led by a first secretary. The National Assembly gives the Welsh more control over their own affairs by assuming functions of the old Welsh Office and allocating the budget approved by the secretary of state for Wales in the British Parliament. The National Assembly also takes on some economic responsibility and promotes Welsh interests in the European Union through the European Parliament.

Unlike the Scottish Parliament, the National Assembly is not able to raise taxes, and the British Parliament in London remains the primary lawmaker for Wales. However, the National Assembly is able to make secondary legislation, the rules and regulations that fill in the framework set out in the Acts of Parliament. The British government continues to be responsible for key areas such as foreign affairs, defense, taxation, overall economic policy, and social security.

Votes being counted in the Ceredigion constituency during the 2010 general election.

POLITICAL PARTIES IN WALES

All the main British political parties (the Labour Party, the Liberal Democrats, and the Conservatives) are active in Wales, as is Plaid Cymru. The Labour Party has a strong following among the Welsh. Prior to World War I, the Liberal Party was the most popular political party in Wales. During World War I, men as well as women were involved in Britain's war effort, which was led by a Welsh prime minister named David Lloyd George. The war and its aftermath, however, changed the political climate in Wales. At the end of the war, Wales went into an economic depression, and many people lost their jobs. The Liberal Party began losing support, and many Welsh began voting for Labour, which stood for nationwide solidarity and the interests of working people. This shift was particularly noticeable in the industrialized south. The Liberal Party remained popular in parts of rural Wales, but eventually attitudes became predominantly Labour.

Between 1999 and 2007 there have been three elections for the National Assembly. Labour won the largest share of votes and seats in each election, either as a minority administration or in coalition, first with the Liberal Democrats and more recently with Plaid Cymru. The Labour Party currently holds 26 seats in the 60-seat assembly, followed by Plaid, which has 15 seats.

The party leader of Plaid Cymru, Ieuan Wyn Jones addressing the audience at the party's 2010 spring conference in Cardiff.

DAVID LLOYD GEORGE (1863-1945)

David Lloyd George is perhaps the most famous Welsh politician. He was born to Welsh parents and raised in a small village in north Wales. He was charismatic and eloquent, which made him popular with voters and attractive to women. The media nicknamed him the "Welsh Wizard" because of his full cloak, wide-brimmed hat, flowing hair, full mustache, and twinkling eyes.

His achievements were many, including laying the foundations for the welfare state and leading Great Britain to victory in World War I by reorganizing the munitions industry. During the course of his political career, Lloyd George was a Liberal minister of Parliament, chancellor of the Exchequer, and prime minister of Great Britain from 1916 to 1922. Toward the end of his life, he was made an earl.

NATIONALISM AND PLAID CYMRU

In 1925 a group of academics headed by Saunders Lewis established the Welsh Nationalist Party, or Plaid Cymru. Currently committed to achieving political independence for Wales as a "region" within the European Union, in its early days its central aim was to protect the Welsh language. It was seen more as a pressure group and made little headway until the by-elections of 1966, when Gwynfor Evans won the first Plaid Cymru seat in Parliament. This moved the party beyond the issue of language into mainstream politics, where it became a nationalist alternative to the Labour Party.

Plaid Cymru's support has always been strongest in the rural Welsh-speaking areas of central and western Wales. In recent years leaders of the party have pushed for votes outside the traditional areas, increasing the party's following. The party's philosophy has also developed in a more outward-looking and European direction. There are other movements on the periphery of Plaid Cymru, some of which strive for independence based on

cultural and linguistic differentiation. Some of these movements, such as the Welsh Language Society and Meibion Glyndŵr, have resorted to using various methods of civil disobedience.

Soldiers marching in a parade on Armed Forces Day.

JUSTICE AND THE LAW

Wales has the same system of justice as England, and there are two kinds of courts. Most cases are dealt with by magistrates' courts, and every town has one of these. Magistrates (or justices of peace) are not usually trained lawyers but are appointed by a local committee. A panel of magistrates can decide whether someone is guilty of a crime and can also impose punishment. Even serious crimes are heard in a magistrates' court before they are referred to a higher court, which in most cases is a crown court, where the judge is a professional lawyer and there is a jury of 12 people who decide on a verdict. There is also the Court of Appeal of England and Wales to which a convicted person can apply, and the highest court in Britain is the House of Lords.

Overall control of the police force rests with the British government in London, but local police forces enforce the law. Although Wales does not have any independent defense arrangements, it does have three regiments that serve in the British army: the Welsh Guards, the Royal Welsh Fusiliers, and the Royal Regiment of Wales.

ECONOMY

**Shoppers inside one of Cardiff's vibrant shopping arcades.
Shops such as these help to keep the Welsh economy healthy.**

CHAPTER 4

DURING THE 18TH and 19th centuries, the Welsh economy moved from dependence on agriculture to dependence on heavy industry, particularly coal mining. In the second half of the 20th century, the coal industry collapsed, causing large-scale unemployment and forcing the economy to restructure.

Heavy industry has all but disappeared, and Wales now has a more modern economy, dominated by high-technology manufacturing and services.

Wales has left behind its industrial past, and today the economy is dominated by small manufacturing industries and the service sector.

Workers at a textile warehouse in Wales.

INDUSTRY IN THE PAST

Prior to the 18th century, most Welsh people made their living by farming, and the wool trade was one of the most bustling. Britain's Industrial Revolution had a profound effect on the economy of Wales. The workforce shifted from farming to factory-based industries, and from rural to industrial areas. Southwestern Wales became an important center for the copper industry, while the valleys in southern Wales (particularly Merthyr Tydfil) had some of the largest ironworks. In the northeast and northwest of Wales, iron, copper, slate, and lead were mined.

Between 1840 and 1920, valleys in southern Wales produced vast quantities of coal, which became the dominant industry, although steel and tin were also important. Wales became a major exporter of coal, and the Rhondda Valley became world renowned. A steady production of coal was maintained until the 1950s, when the availability of substitutes and cheaper imports made the coalpits uneconomical. From the 1960s onward, the pits began to close. The last pit in the Rhondda Valley closed in 1990. Today coal mining and slate quarrying have disappeared, although Wales is still an important center for steel.

The Port Talbot steelworks in Wales.

LAURA ASHLEY

Laura Mountney was born in 1925 in Merthyr Tydfil, south Wales. Her family moved to London, but Laura was sent back to Wales to escape the air raids during World War II. In 1949 she married and became Laura Ashley.

While a secretary in London, she started designing her own floral patterns and printed them on tea towels with a printing machine designed by her husband. Many people liked her towels, so she moved back to Wales and opened a factory in Machynlleth in 1963. As her business expanded, she began making long dresses with flower patterns and opened more factories. Before long, Ashley had opened shops throughout the United Kingdom, France, the United States, and Australia. She died in 1985 after falling down the stairs, but her creative talent lives on in her designs, which are still sold around the world.

INDUSTRY TODAY

To combat the negative effects of the collapse of the coal industry, the British government developed a policy to encourage new industries such as electronics, engineering, manufacturing, and car assembly to establish themselves in Wales. This policy has been partially successful: Ford has maintained an engine production plant at Bridgend since 1980, which has recently received extra investment. Electronics is a major growth area, with many North American, Japanese, and European companies investing in small and midsize operations.

Metal-ore refining is a long-established industry in Wales, and today there are major facilities in many of the larger towns, such as Port Talbot, Newport, and Caerphilly. Most of the tinplate and aluminum produced in the UK comes from Welsh plants. There are also two oil refineries at Milford Haven, which process around two-fifths of the UK's petroleum.

SERVICE SECTOR

Although growth in the service sector has been significant in banking and finance, business services, and self-employment, Wales still lags behind the rest of the UK in these areas, with fewer of these high-value services than other parts of Britain. Most service jobs in Wales are in the public sector, in areas such as health, education, and public administration. The public sector is a major employer in Wales, employing almost 380,000 people (28 percent of the workforce). Most service-sector jobs are centered on Cardiff, the capital, and nearby Swansea.

TOURISM

Tourism generates upward of $4.5 billion in revenue each year, making it an important part of the economy. More than 11 million tourists visit Wales every year to enjoy its beautiful landscape and relaxed way of life. Most tourists make the short journey from neighboring England; overseas visitors come primarily from the United States, Ireland, and Germany. The tourist sector employs roughly 100,000 people, or 8 percent of all employees in Wales.

More than a century old, the Snowdon Mountain Railway steam train is the only public rack and pinion railway in the British Isles. Wales is known as a mecca for railway enthusiasts.

The unique Tourist Information Centre in Cardiff Bay.

Tourism is a flourishing sector of the economy because of the country's natural beauty and the lure of its castles and legends. There are rugged mountains, cool forests, mysterious lakes, a wonderful coastline, and countless quaint towns. Wales has everything a nature lover could want. Hill walking, hiking, canoeing, hang gliding, kayaking, and climbing are all very popular activities in the national parks. Historical sites are also good business. Apart from museums, there are more than 100 impressive castles to explore, as well as Roman forts and settlements, Christian monasteries, and the remains of a romantic Celtic past. Many of these places are preserved by Cadw, the historic-environment service of the Welsh Assembly government.

Visitors can also relive the past by riding on one of the Great Little Trains, narrow-gauge steam trains that chug through some of the most scenic parts of the countryside. Many of these trains are more than 100 years old and once transported coal and slate. Even abandoned mines now attract visitors with an interest in industrial archaeology. At the Big Pit: National Coal Museum at Blaenavon and at the Rhondda Heritage Park, ex-miners show tourists how the mines once worked and tell them gripping tales of the past.

A government body, the Welsh Development Agency, is responsible for promoting Wales as a place in which to invest.

FARMING

More than 4 million acres (1.6 million ha) of the land in Wales—about three-quarters of the total—are devoted to agriculture. There are many small family farms, and livestock farming accounts for about 85 percent of their output because of the climate and poor soil conditions. The average farm size is 74 to 99 acres (30 to 40 ha), which is small by UK standards. Roughly 55,000 people are directly employed in farming.

Farmers in the highland areas rear cattle and sheep, whereas the lowlands are dairy farming country. On arable land, farmers grow wheat, barley, oats, vegetables, and potatoes. The arable sector accounts for just 10 percent of total output. Pembrokeshire, in the southwest, has particularly good land. It is often called the Garden of Wales because everything from honey to potatoes is grown or cultivated there.

FISHING AND FORESTRY

The Welsh fishing industry is the smallest in the UK, employing just slightly more than 1,000 fishermen full-time. The southern shores are abundant

A flock of sheep grazing on a farm in northern Wales against the backdrop of the Clwydian Hills.

with cockles, which women used to sell door-to-door in the villages. Inland, in the southwest, people used to fish from coracles, boats light enough for fishermen to carry home. These boats are still used to fish for salmon in the River Teifi, and some villages hold coracle races in summer.

Many of the forests in Wales are planted and managed by the Forestry Commission. Most of the trees, such as the dark green conifers, have been planted for timber and do not provide a natural habitat for birds and animals. After public debate, more consideration is now being given to preserving the environment. In some areas the majestic old oak, ash, and beech trees have been preserved.

Welsh fishermen at sea.

WORKING

At 7.5 percent, the unemployment rate in 2009 was 2.2 percent higher than in 2008, partly a consequence of the recession that lasted from 2008 to 2010. During the past decade, increased employment opportunities in manufacturing and services and through self-employment have offset job losses in heavy industry. By and large, cities such as Cardiff and Swansea and the towns of the northern and southern coastal belts have experienced the greatest increases in employment, whereas the former industrial towns of the valleys of southern Wales have suffered the greatest unemployment. Distant from other economic centers, many of the former industrial towns of southern and western Wales are among the poorest areas in the European Union. Wages and living standards are highest in the capital, Cardiff. The city benefits from good road and rail connections to nearby Bristol in England and on to London.

Office workers having a discussion at a meeting in Wales.

As the economy continues to move away from farming, Wales faces the problem of rural depopulation. To combat this, the government is trying to attract young people back to rural areas. The Development Board for Rural Wales was set up in 1977 to attract businesses to the mainly rural area of mid-Wales.

There was an influx of women into the workforce during the two World Wars, when women took over traditionally "male" jobs in the factories while the men were away at war. During the consumer boom of the 1950s and 1960s, more jobs became available for women. There was also an increasing acceptance of a woman's dual role as wife/mother and career woman. However, although more women are working, they still on average earn less than men and are underrepresented in management.

SHOPPING

In Wales the "high street" is usually the main shopping area in towns and cities. Most large towns have major supermarkets, such as Tesco, and department stores, such as Marks & Spencer. In recent years there has been an increase in the number of big retail parks built on the outskirts of larger towns and cities. These cater to the increasing consumer demand for one-stop shopping and carry everything from food to housewares and from clothing to hardware. Shopping habits in smaller villages have changed less quickly, however, and people are still more likely to buy from their local butcher and baker.

Most neighborhoods have a corner shop. Corner shops sell some food, but their main business is selling newspapers, cigarettes, and other small items. On Sunday people will pop out to the corner shop to pick up the newspaper and a pint of milk. Shopkeepers usually know their local customers by name and enjoy chatting with them.

TRANSPORTATION

Highways and bridges link the major industrial and residential centers in Great Britain. The Severn bridges are the gateway to southern Wales from England. When the first bridge was built in 1966, it was one of the longest single-span arches in the world. Traffic across this bridge was so heavy that later on, a second bridge had to be built just a few miles downstream in 1996.

Although automobiles have largely replaced rail travel, trains are still a pleasant and efficient way to travel in Wales. Fast trains connect Welsh cities and towns to each other and the rest of Great Britain. Most major English cities have direct rail connections to Wales via Cardiff Central Station. Cardiff is also the center of an urban rail network, linking to more than 80 stations in the area.

The Menai Suspension Bridge, designed by the great road builder Thomas Telford, connects the Isle of Anglesey with the mainland. The bridge was completed in 1826. Trains also run direct from London to the port of Holyhead on Anglesey, where ferries link the British mainland to Dublin in Ireland.

The main airport in Wales is in Cardiff, the entry point for all international tourist flights. Not all international airlines fly directly to Cardiff, however, and it is sometimes just as easy for international travelers to fly into London in England and then take the train to Cardiff, a journey of roughly two hours.

With such a long coastline, it is not surprising that Wales has many seaports. Ferries travel from Ireland to Holyhead and the picturesque town of Fishguard. Other ports, such as Cardiff, Newport, Swansea, and Barry, handle mainly cargo. The port at Milford Haven is one of the leading centers in Western Europe for importing and refining oil.

The old and new Severn bridges connect England and Wales over the Severn River estuary.

ENVIRONMENT

The deep orange sunset shines over green seaweed-covered rocks at Penmon Point on the Isle of Anglesey in Wales.

WALES IS FACING THE SAME environmental challenges as many other countries around the world. These include dealing with the devastating effects of climate change and global warming, such as coastal erosion and flooding.

The Welsh Assembly government and environmental groups are constantly trying to find better ways to manage, reduce, and reuse waste as well as tackle the problems of dwindling energy supplies by developing renewable energy.

Some of the main environmental problems affecting Wales today are coastal erosion, flooding, and the sourcing of greener forms of energy such as wind power.

Beautiful wildflowers lead the way to the South Stack lighthouse in Wales.

In Wales there are particular concerns over how the environment affects the stunning scenery of the national parks and the long and beautiful coastline that surrounds a large area of Wales. Tourism is a significant industry, and looking after the environment will help Wales not just protect this sector of its economy but also preserve its natural beauty for future generations.

CHANGES IN THE NATIONAL PARKS

The Welsh are justifiably proud of their stunning national parks. Together the national parks make up one-fifth of the total area of Wales. They are home to important wildlife and rare flora and fauna. The national parks are a vital resource to Wales, as they attract a high number of tourists and visitors every year who come to appreciate their natural beauty. The national parks are especially important to southern Wales, which depends on them for its supply of drinking water.

The spectacular Green Bridge of Wales is a natural arch that was carved by the sea into the cliffs of Saint Govan's along the Pembrokeshire Coast National Park.

As certain parts of the national parks experience extreme temperatures and include some of Wales's highest and lowest points, these areas are particularly vulnerable to the effects of climate change. One effect of climate change has been a sharp increase in rainfall, which has contributed to heavy flooding in some areas. Other negative consequences include soil erosion, droughts, and storms.

As a result of both climate change and global warming, other parts of the national parks have experienced hotter and longer summers. This dryness has resulted in and will continue to cause devastating fires that destroy wildlife and flora, even threatening some species with extinction.

Warmer winter temperatures have started to affect the natural balance of the national parks. Animals that would otherwise have perished in more severe winter conditions will thrive in the milder climate. This means an overall increase in the number of animals, which will ultimately lead to a situation whereby there will be less food for all.

The people who live and farm the lands within the national parks are also victims of this environmental change. It has always been a challenge to farm these lands, but today they are finding it increasingly difficult to make a living from land savaged by the harsh effects of climate change.

Morning sunshine illuminates the patchwork fields in the Usk Valley of Brecon Beacons National Park. The Black Mountains can be seen in the distance as well.

Ramsey Island lies just off the coast of the Saint David's Peninsula. Rich with cliffs and heathland, the island has been made a nature reserve.

Another victim of environmental change includes the upland moors of the Mynydd Du, also known as the Black Mountains, which are part of Brecon Beacons National Park. These moorlands have suffered from the destructive effects of burning and pollution as well as overgrazing. They have seen their flora and fauna deteriorate rapidly over the years. Plants such as cotton grasses, heather, and sphagnum moss, which could previously be found growing in abundance, are now failing to thrive in these areas.

Industrial pollution and overgrazing have contributed to dangerous levels of soil erosion within large areas of the national parks, particularly where peat is found. When peat is exposed through activities such as burning, cutting, or erosion, it produces unwanted greenhouse gases. To stop the negative effects of climate change and protect the national parks for future generations, the authorities and environmental groups are encouraging farmers to alter the way they work, paying particular attention to the problem of overgrazing.

To help the farmers in their battle against the effects of soil erosion, the authorities have invested in projects in certain parts of the national parks to restore moorlands and peat areas that have been damaged. It is hoped that the restoration work will allow mosses and other plants to grow again to help prevent the further erosion of precious soil.

It is not every day that a small country like Wales makes headlines around the world. It did in February 1996, however, when the oil tanker Sea Empress *spilled 76,000 tons (69,000 metric tons) of oil into the sea just off the Pembrokeshire coast.*

A major cleanup operation of the oil-covered rocks and beaches ensued to minimize the damage to tourism. But the environment will take longer to restore. The spill killed an entire population of rare starfish, and it will be years before the ecological system returns to normal.

In 2002 a tanker carrying about 90,000 tons (81,648 metric tons) of crude oil spilled some of its cargo en route to Milford Haven, again along the Pembrokeshire coast in western Wales. Thankfully, only a small volume of its cargo was spilled.

FLOODING AND COASTAL EROSION

The impact of climate change and global warming is being felt particularly along the stunning coastlines of Wales. It is believed that 75 percent of Wales's precious coastline could be in jeopardy during the next century if plans are not put in place to tackle the growing problem of flooding and coastal erosion.

Changes in the climate have produced more flooding, more dramatic storms, and a rise in sea levels, which in turn have caused much of the coast to erode. In severely affected areas, parts of the coast have even begun to disappear. It is critical that initiatives are implemented quickly to prevent further coastal erosion, as many people in Wales live near the coast, and the Welsh tourism industry relies heavily on the survival of its beautiful coastline. The disappearance of the coastline will also affect the unique flora and fauna found there.

A sleepy bay off Porthdinllaen in northern Wales.

Both the Welsh Assembly government and the National Trust, which owns approximately 145 miles (233 km) of the Welsh coastline, are working hard to raise public awareness of the dangers faced by the coastline. Ultimately the whole community as well as the authorities will have to work together to reduce the overall carbon footprint in order to save the coastline from further erosion. The challenge is to find more innovative ways to manage the problems of rising sea levels beyond simply building concrete sea defenses, a solution that some experts find unsatisfactory, as it only moves the problem to another area. Besides building flood and sea defenses, the authorities have plans to build resilience in buildings and better prepare communities by ensuring that there are effective strategies in place in the event of severe flooding. The government can also work to establish effective legislation that will help control coastal erosion and prevent the situation from worsening.

It has been estimated that by 2080, the sea levels along the coastline of Wales will increase by as much as 28 inches (71 cm). If this does indeed happen, Wales could lose many of its wonderful beaches, coastal plants and animals, traditional seaside villages, medieval churches, intricate dune systems, historic forts, important archaeological monuments, and much more. The pretty coastal village of Porthdinllaen in northern Wales is already living with the effects of coastal erosion and rising sea levels. During high tide, water reaches some of its houses, including its famous inn and lifeboat station.

Places and monuments at risk as a result of coastal erosion are:

- *Cemlyn Lagoon—A brackish lagoon, separated from Cemlyn Bay by a shingle beach, this is an important wildlife site, habitat to a population of terns and other wildlife. It was designated a Site of Special Scientific Interest in 1958 and is part of the Anglesey Heritage Coast and the Isle of Anglesey's Area of Outstanding Natural Beauty.*

- *Marloes Sands—This vast and remote beach in Pembrokeshire's southern peninsula is a popular destination for locals and tourists alike, yet it remains relatively peaceful throughout the year. The coastal footpath offers fantastic views of the beach, Skokholm Island, and Gateholm Island.*

- *Stackpole Estate—An area in Pembrokeshire of beautiful sandy beaches, lakes, wooded valleys, and important archaeological sites, it is best known as the home of the famous Bosherston lily ponds. It is also a haven for otters, choughs, and waterfowl.*

- *Dinas Dinlle—Designated a Site of Special Scientific Interest, this is an Iron Age hill fort in Gwynedd situated on a cliff above a large sand and pebble beach that offers views toward the Lleyn Peninsula and Llanddwyn Island. As a result of coastal erosion, only a double semicircular rampart of the original fort remains. Roman pottery has been discovered in this area.*

- *Nicholaston Burrows—A magnificent isolated beach in Gower, it has grassy sand dunes rich in plant and animal wildlife that are now vulnerable to rising sea levels.*

- *Llanrhidian Marsh—A Site of Special Scientific Interest, this spectacular and extensive area of grazed salt marsh adjoins the Loughor Estuary in Gower. It is home to an important population of waders and wildfowl whose existence is being threatened by rising sea levels.*

- *Rhossili—This famous 5-mile (8-km) stretch of sandy beach with towering cliffs is situated at the tip of the Gower Peninsula. Its breathtaking views include Worm's Head, a path that stretches out to sea and transforms into an island with the advancing tide.*

A wind farm in Anglesey.

The National Trust has warned that within 100 years, 66 of Wales's coastal areas covering more than 6 square miles (15 square km) will be in serious danger of flooding and even disappearing altogether. In 2009, as a response to this serious threat, the Welsh Assembly government invested £38 million ($56 million) in flood and coastal-erosion risk management. In addition, the minister for social justice and local government awarded £500,000 ($740,475) in 2009 to the Fire and Rescue Service in Wales to improve its rescue capability in the event of severe flooding.

WIND ENERGY

The hilly landscape of Wales is ideal for the development of wind farms. Wind power is an extremely clean source of energy because it produces no greenhouse-gas emissions or waste products. As a result, environmental groups including Friends of the Earth Cymru as well as the Welsh Assembly government support the development of both onshore and offshore wind farms to generate renewable energy for Wales. An added economic benefit of building more wind farms is that it will create jobs for the people of Wales.

In 2005, in response to the UK government's energy-policy target of producing 10 percent of its electricity from renewable sources by 2010, the Welsh Assembly government stated that building more onshore wind farms was the only realistic way to achieve this ambitious goal.

Launched in 2005, the Cefn Croes Wind Project, situated on a hillside near Devil's Bridge in Ceredigion in mid-Wales, is the UK's largest and most powerful onshore wind-energy project. It cost £59 million ($87 million) to build, and its 39 wind turbines, rising to a maximum height of 328 feet (100 m), can produce 58.5 megawatts in total, sufficient to supply more than 40,000 homes with electricity. It is estimated that this powerful wind-farm project will save approximately 4 million tons (3.63 million metric tons) of carbon dioxide in total emissions over a 25-year period. As a consequence, many believe powerful wind farms such as this are the future of green energy production. This area of mid-Wales has been called "Europe's wind farm capital" because of its high number of wind farms and turbines: 9 wind farms and 277 turbines.

Another soure of energy comes from the innovative solar center with 176 solar panels and low-energy lights at Baglan Bay Energy Park in Neath, South Glamorgan.

In spite of the clear benefits of developing wind energy, some groups, including the Campaign for the Protection of Rural Wales, oppose the development of more wind farms in Wales. They are concerned about the effect of wind farms on scenery and ecology. Some of this opposition is so fierce that certain wind-farm projects have been blocked. These campaigners are not convinced that the wind farms generate enough energy to justify their development. Instead, they put pressure on the Welsh Assembly government to focus on alternative forms of renewable energy, such as solar power and hydropower. Supporters of wind farms warn that costly and dangerous nuclear power stations would be built in place of wind farms in order to meet the demand for more energy.

RECYCLING AND COMPOSTING

In recent years Wales has begun to make its recycling program a priority. Like many other governments, the Welsh Assembly has realized that recycling is crucial and will benefit the environment as well as the economy in the long run. Wales has made massive improvements in its efforts, recycling approximately 40 percent of its waste in 2009. By way of comparison, in 2003, Wales recycled only around 2 percent of its waste.

In 2009 the government launched a challenging program with a goal of being a "zero waste nation" by 2050; by 2025 Wales is expected to meet a 70 percent target of recycling municipal waste. Other environmentally friendly initiatives that have been undertaken include supplying every household in Cardiff with food- and garden-waste collection once a week, free of charge. Food and garden waste is sent off to separate compositing facilities and recycled accordingly. Cardiff is in fact the first city in the United Kingdom to enjoy this important service, which will help reduce the amount of waste that ends up in landfill sites in Wales.

Colorful recycling bins at the Centre for Alternative Technology in Machynlleth, Powys.

There are approximately 15 landfill sites in Wales, but each one is nearing its maximum capacity. It is estimated that, unless immediate action is taken, these landfill sites will be completely full within 10 years. The good news, however, is that during the past decade, Wales has decreased the greenhouse-gas emissions from these sites by about 50 percent. This has been achieved mainly as a result of stringent European Union (EU) legislation and regulation. The EU has threatened authorities with heavy penalties if they do not meet their landfill targets. The Welsh Assembly government has plans to invest more than £25 million ($37 million) to build a system of anaerobic digestion plants that can instantly process food waste into compost. These new plants can also generate heat, possibly supplying Wales with some electricity at the same time.

Environmental groups in Wales, like others elsewhere, are making people aware that our modern lifestyle of excessive and disposable consumerism takes a heavy toll on the environment. In the past decade or so, Cardiff has seen a remarkable level of regeneration and is today a thriving cultural and commercial hub. Although this has created many jobs and attracted large numbers of tourists, the rapid growth the city has experienced has also caused environmental problems, including an increase in the waste it produces. In Wales waste that cannot be recycled mostly ends up in incinerators. The burning of large amounts of waste is of course detrimental to the environment.

THE WELSH

A family at Lleithyr Meadow Caravan Club site near Saint David's in Pembrokeshire.

> **T**HERE IS SOMETHING UNIQUE about Wales. The people have distinctive accents, and in many areas of Wales, Welsh is spoken as a first language. But what really defines the Welsh is their spirit: passionate, down-to-earth, and warmhearted.

Wales's small ethnic minority population can be found mainly in the cities of Cardiff, Swansea, and Newport.

THE WELSH

The Welsh are descendants of the Celtic Britons. The Celts never established an empire, but by 300 B.C. their Iron Age culture prevailed throughout the British Isles. Successive invaders eventually pushed the Britons into the remote mountainous regions where they maintained their unique culture. Many elements of modern Welsh culture evolved from the culture of the ancient Celts.

The Welsh delight in telling stories, and something as simple as giving travel directions can often be embellished with history, folklore, and the latest local gossip. Their rich and powerful facility with words comes from the language itself, which is rooted in an ancient Celtic culture of myth and legend.

Welsh children in their traditional costumes.

The Welsh enjoy singing. Music is close to the hearts of the people. Whether it is a casual sing-along at the pub or a formal men's choir, the Welsh have a talent for singing. It is no wonder that Wales is often called the Land of Song. The Welsh tradition of male choirs dates from the Industrial Revolution, when the overcrowding of Welsh industrial towns encouraged community events.

POPULATION

Only about 3 million people live in Wales, a mere 5 percent of the population of the United Kingdom. In fact, there are about twice as many sheep as there are people in Wales. For historical reasons, two-thirds of the population is concentrated in the south, in the cities of Cardiff, Swansea, and Newport, where the population is also more anglicized than in the north.

As a once heavily industrialized region, southern Wales attracted many immigrants in search of economic opportunities. From 1901 to 1911, immigrants arrived here at a faster rate than to any other country, with the exception of the United States. They came from other parts of Great Britain and other European countries such as Italy and Poland.

Teenagers hanging out together in Wales.

Bertrand Russell is one of the most renowned logicians and philosophers of the 20th century. He was born in Trellech in Gwent, south Wales, but lived most of his life in England.

He published many books, having at one time more than 40 books in print, covering philosophy, mathematics, science, education, history, religion, and politics. His three-volume Principia Mathematica *(1910, 1912, and 1913), which he co-authored with Alfred North Whitehead, was immensely influential. In 1950 he won the Nobel Prize in literature.*

During World War I his activities as a pacifist resulted in his being fined £100 in 1916, dismissed from his lectureship at Trinity College, and imprisoned for six months in 1918. In 1954 he made his famous "Man's Peril" broadcast on the British Broadcasting Corporation (BBC) condemning the Bikini H-bomb tests. He also set up the International War Crimes Tribunal to publicize alleged American atrocities in Vietnam. At the age of 83, Russell returned to Wales, where he remained until his death.

THE WELSH IN AMERICA

In the 17th century groups of Welsh people went to America to escape persecution for their religious beliefs. Many of them made what later became the state of Pennsylvania their home. Here they tried, unsuccessfully, to establish a Welsh utopia called Cambria, the ancient Roman name for Wales. Many people also went to America to look for economic opportunities. The Welsh coal miners and steelworkers who arrived in Pennsylvania in the 19th century helped to establish the coal and steel industries there.

ROBERT OWEN (1771-1858)

Robert Owen was a socialist held in high esteem by his countrymen. Born in Newton, Montgomeryshire, he left Wales to work in the cotton trade in Manchester. He worked his way up to the position of mill manager and became incredibly wealthy.

Owen was a kind employer who believed in social equality. He started the cooperative movement based on the premise that both consumers and workers would receive mutual benefits. He established an experimental workers' community in New Lanark, Scotland. In 1821 he set up a second model community in New Harmony, Indiana, in the United States. Here he established a free public library, a kindergarten, and a free public school.

He finally returned to Newton, where he died in 1858. The original furnishings from his home can now be seen in a memorial museum there.

People of Welsh extraction have distinguished themselves in America. John Llewellyn Lewis became the well-known leader of the United Mine Workers of America, and there have been six U.S. presidents of Welsh extraction: Thomas Jefferson, James Monroe, Abraham Lincoln, Andrew Jackson, Richard Nixon, and Calvin Coolidge.

CLASS

Welsh society is not classless, but the social differences are not as obvious as in England. In England a person's accent is often the most obvious sign of social class, and regional accents have traditionally been associated with the working class.

JOHN LLEWELLYN LEWIS (1880-1969)

Born in Iowa to immigrant parents from Welsh mining towns, John Llewellyn Lewis had to work in the coal mines from the age of 15. Starting as the head of a United Mine Workers of America (UMWA) local in 1911, he later became the president of UMWA from 1920 to 1960.

A giant among American leaders in the first half of the 20th century, Lewis was an adviser to presidents and a challenger to corporate leaders. A man of imposing appearance, with overhanging brows and a bulldog chin, Lewis was fond of using literary allusions and harsh epithets in his speeches. One of his speeches went: "I have pleaded your case from the pulpit and from the public platform—not in the quavering tones of a feeble mendicant asking alms, but in the thundering voice of the captain of a mighty host, demanding the rights to which free men are entitled."

Lewis helped to raise living standards for millions of Americans through his work in organizing industrial workers through the Congress of Industrial Organizations in the 1930s. He set up the UMWA Welfare and Retirement Fund, which improved health care for miners in the United States. He retired in early 1960s. In 1964 President John Kennedy awarded Lewis the Presidential Medal of Freedom, the nation's highest civilian decoration.

In Wales, however, accents denote regional rather than social differences, and it is more difficult to determine a person's social background from his or her accent. The main reason for this is historical. When Wales was united with England (under the Acts of Union), members of the Welsh aristocracy moved to England, and the landlords who stayed behind became anglicized. They spoke English and felt closer to the English than to the majority of Nonconformist Welsh speakers. Hence the ordinary people were able to produce their own leaders, preachers, poets, and teachers and to establish their own social hierarchy.

LIFESTYLE

A family walking alongside the
Talybont Reservoir in Wales.

>T HE WELSH ARE A PATRIOTIC
people with a rich cultural heritage
and a tradition of quality education
at all levels. Although the lifestyle in
Wales is still mainly rural, it is becoming
increasingly urbanized.

The Welsh are
proud of their
national identity,
and they enjoy
strong community
and family ties.

FAMILIES

In the old days, a family was a large collection of people who might live
in the same town or village for generations. In many traditional Welsh
families, grandmothers and grandfathers were very influential in a
child's life and helped to reinforce values taught by the parents.

Three generations of family enjoying a picnic on the beach.

Today Welsh families are increasingly fragmented. Economic pressure has made it harder for families to all live in the same area, and grown-up children often leave their hometowns because they cannot find a suitable job there. Nevertheless, family ties are still important, and relatives get together on weekends and special occasions.

A woman's traditional role in the family was that of a wife and mother. Nowadays in Wales, as in many other countries, women are wives and mothers as well as career women. According to the Office for National Statistics, 68 percent of women in Wales were either working or looking for work in the 2001—2002 time period. The increase in the number of working women has meant that couples tend to have fewer children—the average is 2.5 children—and to have their first child later in life. There are also now more single mothers.

A mother helps her toddler take her first steps in the National Botanic Garden of Wales.

Terrace houses in the Rhondda Valley of Wales.

HOUSING

Welsh houses are built in a variety of styles and from a range of materials. In the country there are quaint cottages built of stone and slate that were once mined in the local quarries. In cities such as Cardiff, there are semidetached houses built of brick and modern materials.

Many cities and towns also have public housing, or council houses, that tenants can rent from the local council at a reasonable price. These were originally built for those who could not afford to buy a house, but today tenants have the option to buy their home from the council. There is a limited supply of public housing, and there are some people who can neither afford to rent privately nor obtain council accommodation. Organizations such as Shelter give advice to the homeless and try to increase public awareness about this problem. Across Wales, the Welsh Assembly government is responsible for the provision of new houses as well as the improvement of existing housing conditions.

RURAL SETTLEMENT

Wales is a predominately rural country. There are a few towns and cities, but many picturesque villages are dotted across the countryside. The names of many villages, such as Llangybi in Gwynedd, northern Wales, start with the prefix llan, *meaning "church." A typical Welsh village has a church surrounded by quaint cottages or small houses. There is usually a store, a post office, and a pub where villagers can share a pint or two of beer and exchange news and gossip.*

Inevitably village life has changed. One of the consequences of rural depopulation was that English buyers purchased empty country houses and farms for use as second homes. Of course this diluted local communities, but it also injected money and new skills into them. Nevertheless there was some hostility toward the influx of the English, and extremist groups such as the Sons of Glyndwr set more than 130 second homes on fire during the late 1970s and throughout the 1980s.

The Royal Gwent
Hospital in Newport.

HEALTH CARE

The Welsh are getting healthier, and the life expectancy for men and women is 77 and 81 years respectively. Doctors in Wales have to deal with many cases of former miners who have developed respiratory diseases such as bronchitis and emphysema.

Up until the early part of the 20th century, people in some parts of Wales would consult the village "wise man," who used a number of charms to cure diseases. Children with whooping cough were supposed to make three visits to the wise man, and on each visit the child would eat a cake specially prepared to cure the ailment.

Today health care in Wales is provided through the National Health Service (NHS). It is administered by local authorities and available to all people who register with a doctor near their home. Treatment is free, but there is a charge for prescriptions, although there are exemptions for the elderly. One of the most critical issues concerning the NHS is the waiting time for operations. NHS patients might have to wait a year or more if they need a nonurgent operation. Some people opt for private medical insurance plans with companies such as the British United Provident Association (BUPA).

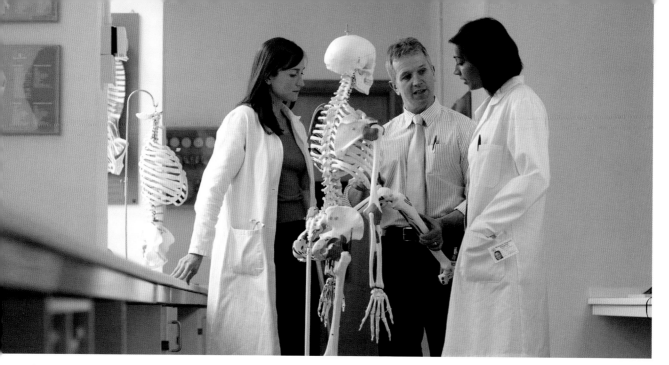

A medical lecturer and his students at Swansea University in Wales.

In Great Britain working people contribute a portion of their salary toward the National Insurance Scheme. This money finances social benefits such as health care, unemployment benefits, and old-age pensions. The government pension is low, and Great Britain's aging population puts additional pressure on the social-security system. As a consequence, more people are making their own pension arrangements to ensure that they will have enough money to live on when they retire.

EDUCATION TODAY

Education is free and compulsory for Welsh children between the ages of 5 and 16. The Department for Education and Employment is responsible for the overall organization of education in England and Wales. The Welsh Assembly in Cardiff shares the responsibility of planning local syllabi with the Local Education Authorities (LEAs).

In the late 1980s, a national curriculum—a set of national learning objectives—was introduced to raise the standard of education in Wales and the rest of Great Britain. English, mathematics, and science are core subjects. Other subjects include geography, history, music, art, technology, physical education, and information technology, and in secondary school,

WELSH NOT

At one time there was prejudice against the Welsh language and a bias toward the use of English. The notorious "Welsh Not" plaque, a wooden sign with the words "Welsh Not" carved on it, used to be hung around the neck of any pupil who was caught speaking Welsh. In 1847 an inflammatory report concerning the state of education was released that virulently attacked the standard of education in Wales and branded Welsh the "language of slavery." It advised against using the Welsh language in schools and recommended more teaching in English. This outraged the Welsh and sparked a storm of controversy, which stimulated the drive for more schools and for free and compulsory education. It also fueled the campaign for more Welsh in education. Today it is evident that the government grants provided to improve the standard of education in the Welsh language have been successful.

for students ages 11 and up, a foreign language. Since 2000, the teaching of the Welsh language has been compulsory in all schools. In the 2008—2009 academic year, 22 percent of classes in primary schools used Welsh as the sole or main medium of instruction. The majority of these Welsh-speaking schools are found in the north and west of the country.

A teacher conducts lessons for her year 3 class in Welsh.

Welsh children go to school from Monday to Friday, and the school day usually begins at 9 A.M. and finishes at 3:30 P.M. The children have about an hour for lunch, and they can either go home or eat at school. Parents can pack lunch or pay for their child to have a hot lunch at school, and if they are poor, lunch will be provided free of charge.

The number of people enrolled in higher education is increasing. About 14 percent of men and 12 percent of women have a degree, with Cardiff having the highest proportion of degree holders at 22 percent. Students can receive Welsh-based education at colleges and at the University of Wales. Vocational education and training is also becoming more popular with young adults, and this is playing an important role in the economic regeneration of Wales.

IMPORTANT EDUCATIONAL INFLUENCES

Education has always been highly valued in Wales, although not widely available. Many working people of the past had little formal education but were known to read voraciously to educate themselves.

School pupils take part in a workshop.

Owain Glyndŵr (also known as Owen Glendower) is one of the greatest heroes in Welsh history. Born of noble Welsh lineage, he was a landowner who was educated in England. His noble birth gave Glyndŵr credibility in the eyes of his countrymen, and he eventually led his people in a national revolt against the English. His bitter struggle began in 1400. By 1404 he had won control over most of Wales by forming alliances with King Henry IV's chief opponents.

Glyndŵr managed to capture Harlech Castle and to form a parliament there and at Machynlleth. He had great plans for a Welsh nation, including the independence of the Welsh church from Canterbury and the creation of two universities. He did not live to implement many of his plans, however, and his rebellion, the last major Welsh attempt to throw off English rule, eventually petered out. He was a hero to the Welsh nationalists in the 19th and 20th centuries.

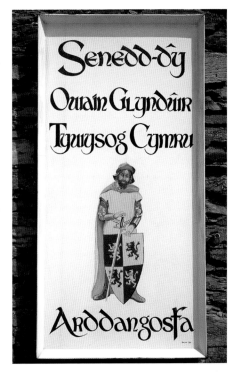

A man who was very influential in the early days of education was Griffith Jones, a minister who in the 18th century organized "traveling schools" (also known as "circulating schools") taught by specially trained preachers who moved from place to place teaching people to read. His efforts helped to make Wales literate. Another important figure of that time, Thomas Charles, brought Sunday schools, which taught reading and writing and encouraged the discussion of theology, to Wales. In the 19th century, two organizations, the British and Foreign Schools Society (established in 1808) and the National Society (established in 1811), started setting up more schools.

In 1870 the Education Act introduced a system of national elementary education, and school attendance was made compulsory by 1880. Local authorities set up "county schools" in 1889 to educate students up to the age of 18, and by 1902 places in these schools were free.

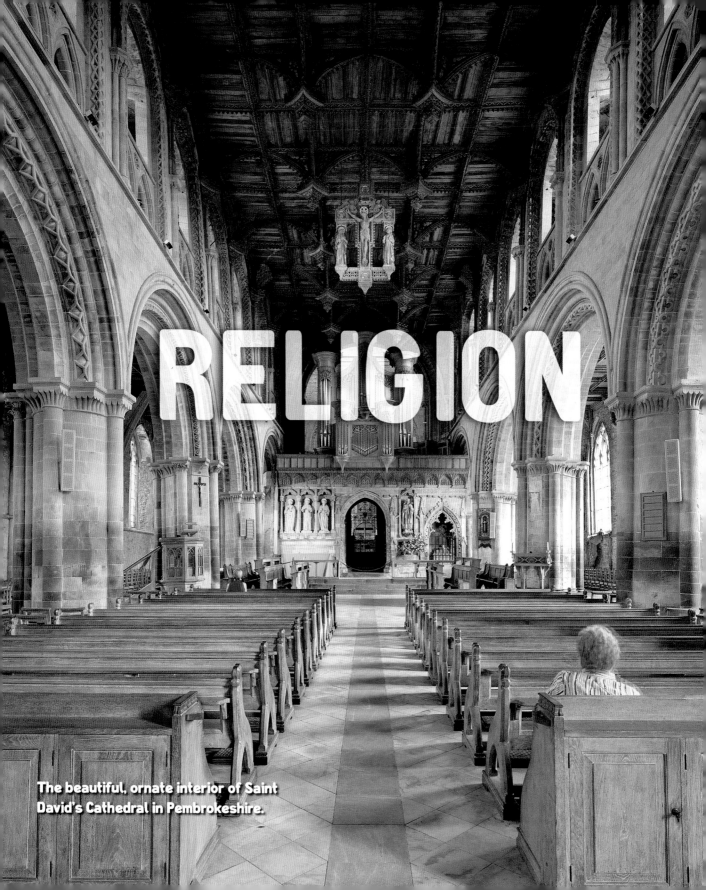

RELIGION

The beautiful, ornate interior of Saint David's Cathedral in Pembrokeshire.

> THE MAJORITY OF WELSH ARE Christians. The Christian religion has many denominations, which differ in emphasis on the main tenets of Christianity. Some of the denominations found in Wales are the Church in Wales (Anglican), Presbyterian, Congregationalist, Roman Catholic, Baptist, Methodist, the Salvation Army, and the Society of Friends.

Non-Christians are in the minority and are concentrated in the cities of Cardiff, Newport, and Swansea. They include Buddhists, Hindus, Jews, Sikhs, and Muslims.

According to the 2001 census, 72 percent of Welsh people declare themselves to be Christians. The majority are members of the Presbyterian Church of Wales.

Saint David's Cathedral, named after Wales's patron saint, dates from the 12th century.

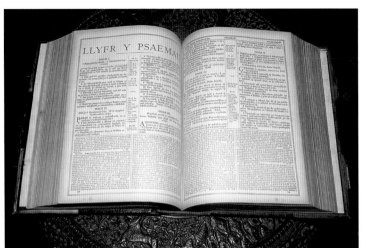

A Welsh Bible dating from 1880. Bishop Morgan's Welsh translation in 1588 greatly influenced the spread of the Welsh language.

THE AGE OF SAINTS

After the Romans left, Wales entered a period marked by frequent wars and a disintegration of urban life. This time period has been referred to as the Dark Ages or the Age of Saints. Although the Romans had planted the seeds of Christianity, it was not until traveling Christian missionaries began spreading the faith in the fifth century that the majority of the population converted. These missionaries were called *sancti*, Latin for "saints," and were influential in Wales. They built monasteries, hospices, and churches and were said to have miraculous healing powers. Saint David, who lived in southern Wales in the sixth century, became the patron saint of Wales.

CHRISTIANITY

The Christian church has three main denominations: Protestant, Roman Catholic, and Orthodox. Although church services vary among them, they share certain common beliefs. All Christians believe there is only one God, and that he is the creator and ruler of the universe. They believe that Jesus was the Son of God and the savior of mankind and that the Bible is inspired by God. The Bible is divided into the Old Testament and the New Testament. The Old Testament is a history of the Jewish people and contains the prophecy that a Messiah will come to earth in preparation for the kingdom of God. Christians believe that Jesus is this Messiah. The New Testament was written by Jesus' followers and tells about his life and teachings.

THE ANGLICAN CHURCH

The Anglican Church has the second-largest number of worshipers in Wales. Fewer than 5 percent of the population in Wales are Anglican. Anglicans

Saint David (Dewi in Welsh) is the patron saint of Wales. He was born near Saint Brides Bay, Pembrokeshire, and his mother was a holy woman called Saint Non. Following his education he set up numerous churches throughout southern Wales. More than 50 churches named after him still exist today. He moved the seat of ecclesiastical (church) government from Caerleon to Mynyw, which remains the cathedral city of western Wales. Saint David set up a religious community there that emphasized a frugal lifestyle. Although he lived on bread, herbs, and water, he was reputed to be 6 feet (2 m) tall, handsome, and very strong. He died in A.D. 600, and his last words were, "Be cheerful and keep your faith." The Cathedral of Saint David's, where he is buried, is now a place of pilgrimage, and his feast day is on March 1.

reject the authority of the pope and other aspects of Roman Catholicism. The organization of the Anglican Church is rather hierarchical. Its clergy are called vicars, and the senior clergy members are called bishops. The Church in Wales originated from the Church of England, which used to be the official Welsh state church. In 1920 the Church in Wales severed its ties with the Church of England.

THE ROMAN CATHOLIC CHURCH

Approximately 3 percent of the population in Wales are Roman Catholics, a small but rapidly growing minority, mainly in the northeast. Roman Catholics consider the pope the spiritual head of the church, and any decisions he makes concerning matters of the faith are binding for Catholics. The current pope is Benedict XVI, who is based in Vatican City, an independent state in Rome, Italy, and the spiritual center of the Roman Catholic Church.

MONASTERIES

Wales has many monasteries. In the early days of Christianity, many missionaries, especially those from Brittany, traveled along the western coast, and some of them settled on Caldey Island. The Benedictines established a community there in the 12th century and stayed until the dissolution of the monasteries by Henry VIII in 1538. Today Caldey Island has a community of monks (of the Cistercian Order) who work the land and make perfume from gorse and lavender. This community is virtually secluded from the world. Its monks keep a harsh routine and practice ceaseless devotions. Barely 3 miles (5 km) from one of Wales's most popular seaside resorts, it supports itself by selling its famous perfume in gift shops and by mail order.

Roman Catholics believe that only through the priest can God forgive men for their sins, so they make regular visits to confession, where they confess their sins to the priest and ask for God's forgiveness. All Christians believe in life after death, but only Catholics believe in purgatory, a state between heaven and hell that is a temporary place of purification. Roman Catholics pray to Mary, the mother of Jesus, and most churches have a picture or statue of her. Catholics use rosary beads when they say a special prayer to Mary. The Catholic Church also recognizes many saints.

The Holy Communion service, known as Mass to the Catholics, is one of the most important ceremonies in all Christian churches. It remembers events at Jesus' Last Supper. When Jesus was eating with his disciples, he took some bread, gave thanks, broke it, and gave it to his disciples, saying, "Take and eat; this is my body." Then he took the cup, gave thanks, and offered it to them, saying, "Drink from it, all of you. This is my blood of the covenant, which is poured out for many for the forgiveness of sins." Roman Catholics believe that the bread and wine given by the priest as part of the service really become Christ's body and blood, whereas most Protestants believe that they represent Christ's body and blood on the cross, on which he died to take God's punishment for all people's sins. In Roman Catholic churches, Holy Communion is received at the altar and can be celebrated daily. Other denominations celebrate it only a few times a month and on special occasions such as Christmas.

FREE CHURCHES AND NONCONFORMISTS

Wales has a history of Nonconformism in religion, meaning religious worship that is a reaction against the practices and governance of the mainstream English churches. Although once the official state church in Wales, the Church of England had fallen out of favor with many Welsh people by the 19th century.

Roman Catholics lining up to receive Holy Communion.

Holywell is famous for Saint Winefride's Well, which has been a place of healing and pilgrimage since the seventh century. According to legend, a spring burst forth from the ground where the severed head of a lovely young virgin fell after she was killed for refusing a prince's advances.

There were many reasons for this. One of the most decisive was that the Church of England was seen as being pro-English, politically conservative, and like the Welsh landowners, remote from the ordinary people. As a result, many working people broke away from the established church and joined Nonconformist groups. By 1851, 80 percent of the population was Nonconformist. The largest Nonconformist group, particularly in the rural areas, was the Calvinist Methodists. Other popular groups were the Congregationalists (or Independents), the Baptists, the Wesleyans, and the Salvation Army.

Methodism was introduced to Wales in the mid-18th century in a form similar to Calvinism. Two of the most famous Welsh Methodist preachers were Daniel Rowland and Howell Harris. The Calvinistic Methodists are now a branch of the Presbyterian Church.

The pretty gardens of Saint John's Methodist Church in Colwyn Bay.

Although they are small and Spartan, Welsh chapels have a simple beauty of their own. More important, they stand as a symbol of the nation's religious revival in the 18th century and a reminder of a way of life that has now passed.

In the second half of the 19th century, chapels sprang up all over Wales. So great was the building boom that it was estimated a new chapel was built every eight days. Chapels and their ministers greatly influenced community life and became involved in politics. Great choirs and bands were born under their roofs, and their Sunday schools played an important role in Welsh education and the survival of the Welsh language.

In the 1860s the chapels advocated the temperance movement, which frowned upon alcohol, pubs, and opening shops on Sundays. As a result, fewer Welsh attended chapel services, as they found the preaching too restrictive. By the early 1900s the chapels began losing followers, and by the beginning of this century, the influence of Nonconformist chapels had declined.

Today Nonconformists are usually called members of free churches, and they worship in chapels. Like the Anglicans, they reject the infallibility of the pope and the right of a priest to forgive sins. However, Nonconformists put less emphasis on liturgy than the Anglican Church, and their services are less formal.

IN GREAT BRITAIN
ADMISSION 50p

LANGUAGE

Welsh women, in their traditional wear, enjoying an early morning chat at the Smallest House in Great Britain in Conwy.

I F YOU ARE DRIVING THROUGH WALES, you will see that the road signs and place names appear in both English and Welsh. Everybody in Wales speaks English, and about one-fifth of the population also speak Welsh.

THE WELSH LANGUAGE

Welsh is the oldest living language in Great Britain and is one of six Celtic languages, which belong to the Indo-European family of languages. It evolved from the language of the ancient Britons. Although written Welsh is the standard, there are different regional accents and dialect variations.

Road signs in Wales are usually in both English and Welsh.

Welsh is an ancient language rooted in Celtic culture. Since the establishment of the Welsh Assembly government in 1999, millions of pounds in grants have been provided to promote the Welsh language.

About 611,000 people in Wales speak Welsh. In the north and the west, more than 80 percent of the population speak the language, and the number of Welsh speakers in the south and the east is steadily increasing. The language had been threatened by an ever-increasing exposure to the English language, most significantly during the Industrial Revolution, when there was a great influx of English to work in the Welsh mines. By 1901 English speakers outnumbered Welsh speakers for the first time.

Yet it seems that the Welsh language is destined to survive. According to a survey conducted in 2004 by the Welsh Language Board, the percentage of the population in Wales who are Welsh speakers increased from 18.5 percent in 1991 to 21.7 percent in 2004. There has been a renewed interest in the language, particularly in the anglicized areas of southern Wales. It is now possible to be educated in Welsh from elementary school through to university.

Boys with their selections in the school library. Reading is a very popular activity for many of the Welsh.

THE CAMPAIGN TO SAVE THE LANGUAGE

Pupils reading a Welsh-language magazine in class.

Since the 1960s, both the government and Welsh-language enthusiasts have tried to maintain the language and give it an official status. In 1962 Saunders Lewis, one of the founders of the Plaid Cymru party, delivered a powerful lecture concerning the "fate of the language." This fueled public concern about the language, and a few months later the Welsh Language Society, or Cymdeithas yr Iaith Gymraeg, was founded. It began a series of successful campaigns in the pursuit of bilingualism, and today it is unusual to see road and town signs that are not in both English and Welsh.

Furthermore, legislation in favor of the Welsh language was also introduced. The Welsh Court Act of 1942 gave any person the right to use the Welsh language in any Welsh court where he or she may feel disadvantaged because of the fact that his or her first language is Welsh. In 1967 the Welsh Language Act expanded this right to give Welsh speakers the right to use the Welsh language in court if they so wish. Demands for more legislation to support the rights of Welsh speakers led to a new Language Act (1993) and the Government of Wales Act (1998), which gave the language equal status to English in the public sector. A Welsh Language Board was also established to promote the use of the language. Nowadays most official information in Wales (such as telephone bills and tax forms) is bilingual.

The Welsh language is closer to Breton, which is spoken in Brittany, France, than it is to the Gaelic languages of Ireland and Scotland.

An assortment of Welsh local, regional, and national newspapers.

MEDIA

The growth in Welsh-language media has injected new life into the language. Prior to 1982, Welsh-language television programs were broadcast for only a few hours on BBC and ITV (Independent Television). The government finally yielded to Welsh demands, and S4C (Sianel Pedwar Cymru, or Channel Four Wales) began broadcasting in 1982, stimulating the Welsh film and television industry. Since the digital switchover on March 31, 2010, S4C Digidol is now the main Welsh-language digital broadcaster, with programs available on satellite throughout Wales and the rest of Europe. Other channels include BBC Wales, BBC 2W, and HTV Wales. Cardiff is now one of the most active television production centers in Britain, especially in the area of animation. In addition, BBC Radio Cymru, established in 1977, transmits in Welsh. Other radio stations include BBC Radio Wales, Red Dragon FM, and Real Radio.

Wales has both English and Welsh newspapers. Britain's national newspapers such as the *Independent* and the *Guardian* provide news about Britain and the world. The closest Wales has to a national newspaper is the *Western Mail*, which is written in English, and its weekend counterpart, *Wales on Sunday*. Additionally, there are online English-language newspapers. There are also many local newspapers and magazines that are published entirely in the Welsh language such as *Y Cymro* (*The Welshman*), a weekly newspaper, which also has an online version. Other Welsh-language community newspapers include *Y Dinesydd* (*The Citizen*), which contains local news about what is happening in and around the capital city of Cardiff. Regional newspapers include the *Daily Post, South Wales Echo, and South Wales Evening Post.*

Good morning—Bore da *(BORREH-dah)*

Good afternoon—P'nawn da *(PN-own-dah)*

How are you?—Sut mae? *(SIT-my)*

Welcome—Croeso *(CROY-so)*

Please—Os gwelwch yn dda *(OS-goo-ell-w-ch-un-thah)*

Thank you—Diolch *(DEE-ol-ch)*

Goodbye—Hwyl *(HOO-eel)*

SPEAKING WELSH

The Welsh language may be daunting to a stranger. To non-Welsh speakers, it may seem amazing that anyone can get their tongue around the name of a tiny village in Anglesey: Llanfairpwllgwyngyllgogerychwyrndrobwllllantysilio-gogogoch. With 58 letters, it is believed to be the longest place-name in the world! The name means "Church of Saint Mary in the Hollow by the White Aspen Near the Rapid Whirlpool and Church of Saint Tysilio by the Red Cave."

The Welsh town with the longest name in the world.

An old-fashioned signpost to Llangollen and Hurleston in Wales.

Many place-names, such as Llangollen, begin with the prefix *llan*, which means "church." The double *l* is a little difficult for English speakers to say because there is no English equivalent. If you want to try to say it, put your tongue behind your teeth and blow out to make a sound like *thlan*.

The Welsh language is also full of imaginative first names. Girls have pretty names such as Bronwen, Megan, and Ceri. Boys have names such as Dylan, Aneurin, and Dafydd. There are fewer surnames than in English, so the names Morgan, Jones, Evans, Williams, and Lloyd are quite common. Some surnames contain the prefix *ap* or *ab*, which means "son of." So the name *ab Owain* means "son of Owain."

LETTERS AND SOUNDS

Welsh may not be the easiest language to master, but it helps to know how to pronounce the letters. The Welsh alphabet is similar to the English one, though there are a few differences. There are seven vowels (*a, e, i, o, u, w, y*) instead of five. Most of the vowels have a short and a long sound. For example, the *a* in *tad* (which means "father") is long, as in the word *hard*, and in the word *mam* (which means "mother"), it is short as in *ham*. The language also has lots of adjoining vowels (such as *ae, ai,* and *oe*), and both vowels are pronounced, but the stress is usually on the first.

The numbers one to ten are *un* (EEN), *dau* (DIE), *tri* (TREE), *pedwar* (PEDWAH), *pump* (PIMP), *chwech* (KWECH), *saith* (S-eye-th), *wyth* (OOITH), *naw* (NOW), and *deg* (DAYG).

The Welsh language does not have the consonants *j, k, v, x,* and *z*, but there are some additional ones: *ch, dd, ff, ll, ph,* and *th*. In Welsh, *c* is always hard, so *Cymru* (the Welsh word for Wales) is pronounced "COME-ree." The letter *w* is pronounced as "oo," so the word *drws* (which means "door") is pronounced "droos." The letter *f* is always pronounced like *v*, and the letter *g* is always hard, as in *get*. *Dd* sounds like the letters *th* in *them*, so *yn dda* (which means "good") sounds like "UN thah."

A BIBLIOPHILE'S DREAM

The number of books printed in Welsh soared after printing was introduced to Wales in 1718. Today publishers such as Gomer Press, Y Lolfa, and the University of Wales encourage Welsh writers. The Welsh Books Council was set up in 1961 to encourage Welsh-language publishing. It provides grants to Welsh-language publishers and runs a children's book club.

The small town of Hay-on-Wye has a reputation as the secondhand-book capital of Wales, and it holds a festival of literature every summer. There are bookshops everywhere selling books on all sorts of subjects ranging from general interest to the occult. The town evolved from a market town to a town of books in the 1960s, when Richard Booth set up a books and antiques store. The demand for old books was so great that Booth began snapping up property to set up other bookstores. Even an old castle began selling books! Booth was a colorful character in his own right, and at one stage he declared Hay-on-Wye an independent state, issuing its own passports and currency.

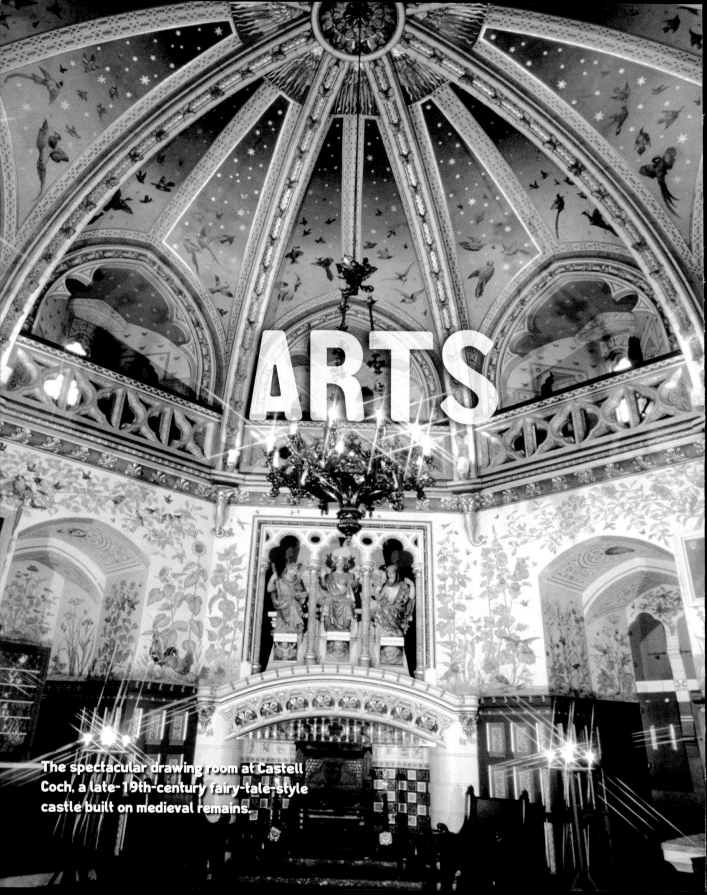

ARTS

The spectacular drawing room at Castell Coch, a late-19th-century fairy-tale-style castle built on medieval remains.

MUSIC AND POETRY ARE ALIVE in the hearts of the Welsh people. This lyrical land has plenty of vibrant men's choirs, sweet-sounding singers, gentle harpists, and imaginative poets. Beyond poetry and music, there are other treasures: gray stone castles, theatrical performers, and a long-standing tradition of craft.

The love of the arts among the Welsh people is especially apparent in their appreciation of music. However, all other forms of art, including literature, dance, film, poetry, architecture, and traditional crafts, are also nurtured in Welsh society.

The majestic Parc Howard Museum near Llanelli in Wales. Best known for its large collection of 19th-century Llanelli pottery, this art gallery also houses paintings and other artworks from the region.

The Wales Millennium Centre in Cardiff is home to the local arts scene. Windows on the front of the building forming the inscription were inspired by Roman classical architecture and bear the inscriptions: "Creu Gwir Fel Gwydr O Ffwrnais Awen" (in Welsh) and "In These Stones Horizons Sing" (in English).

LITERATURE

Wales is a land of myths and legends—of fairies, evil witches, mysterious wizards, and forbidding giants. Many legends spring from *The Mabinogion*, a great medieval collection of Celtic literary texts and folktales.

Beyond magical tales, there is a substantial body of contemporary writing, and many Welsh writers have been published by both English and Welsh companies. Distinguished 20th-century writers include Richard Llewellyn, famous for his work *How Green Was My Valley*; Kate Roberts; Sir Thomas Parry-Williams; Saunders Lewis; and R. Williams Parry. Other successful writers of Welsh origin include Roald Dahl, Dick Francis, and Ken Follett.

POETRY

The Welsh have always had a flair for poetry. Long ago kings such as Hywel the Great paid poets to perform. Known as bards, these poets told magical tales and composed eulogies and elegies for princes and noblemen. Taliesin was a famous sixth-century poet who wrote poems in praise of a king named Urien Rheged.

The bards were elite members of society, and each prince had his own court poet who earned his position through competition at a festival called the *eisteddfod* (ace-DETH-vod). During an *eisteddfod*, contests in poetry, music, and literature were held. Modern poets still compete against each other at the hundreds of *eisteddfodau* (ace-deth-VOD-eye) held in villages and towns throughout Wales. The biggest is the National Eisteddfod of Wales, which is held every year.

Wales has continued to produce outstanding poets. Alun Lewis (1915—44) caught the public's attention with his poems about the grim conditions in the army camps during World War II. Most of his poems in *Raider's Dawn* (1942) and short stories in *The Last Inspection* (1942) are about army life in training camps in England. His most famous poem is "All Day It Has Rained." Another poet of distinction is William Henry Davies (1871—1940). Born in Newport, Davies started out as an apprentice to a picture framer but lived the life of a wanderer, tramping through the United States, losing a foot while trying to jump a train in Canada, and becoming a peddler and street singer in England.

One of the oldest surviving Welsh poems, "Y Gododdin," tells the story of a battle in Yorkshire, which is today part of England. It was composed by a poet known as Aneirin around A.D. 600.

The crowning of the bard at the National Eisteddfod. The archdruid (a former bard himself) places the crown on the winner's head.

Dylan Thomas was born in Swansea in 1914. His father, who was an English teacher, introduced him to literature at a young age. Young Thomas began his career as a newspaper reporter in Swansea. His thirst for adventure took him to London, where he immersed himself in the literary scene. He was a colorful and popular character in the clubs, where he spent many a night conversing with his cronies.

Thomas came from a Welsh-speaking family, but he did not speak any Welsh, which irked some of his fellow Welshmen. Although he was often misunderstood, it is clear from his work that he had a great affection for his country. His poems and stories are distinctively Welsh in their rhythmic quality and draw on his childhood in Wales. His well-known Under Milk Wood *is a popular radio play that delves into the thoughts and lives of a small Welsh seaside community.*

His collection of poems distinguished him as one of the great English-speaking poets of modern times. Dylan's most famous lines are those he wrote for his dying father: "Do not go gentle into that good night/Rage, rage against the dying of light." Dylan himself died at the young age of 39 from an overdose of hard liquor.

His *Autobiography of a Super-Tramp* (1907) appeared with a preface by George Bernard Shaw. He received wide popularity for this and other works, such as *The Loneliest Mountain* (1939). Born in Cardiff, Ronald Stuart Thomas (1913—2000) wrote poetry with a strong cultural and moral consciousness. Another prominent Welsh poet is Dannie Abse, born in Cardiff in 1923 and winner of Wales Book of the Year award in 2008. The most renowned Welsh poet, however, is undoubtedly Dylan Thomas.

MUSIC

The Welsh have a passion for music. For so small a country, there is an incredible reservoir of talent, from opera singers such as the late Sir Geraint Evans, Bryn Terfel, and Dame Margaret Price to pop stars such as Tom Jones and Shirley Bassey.

During the 1970s and 1980s, several rock bands from Wales became popular including the Hellraiser, Budgie, Persian Risk, and Tredegar. Many Welsh rock bands have influenced the campaign to protect the language, including bilingual bands such as Catatonia, which enjoyed international success in the mid- to late 1990s. Other famous Welsh rock bands include Manic Street Preachers and Stereophonics. Charlotte Church found fame at the tender age of 11 years old as a classical singer. She has sold more than 10 million records worldwide. Another talented poet and singer is Twn Morys, who sings for the folk-rock group Bob Delyn a'r Ebillion.

The Welsh have a gift for singing and are world renowned for their men's choirs. Choirs have always been a strong part of popular culture in the valleys. This choral tradition dates back to the 19th century and is still carried on by great choirs such as the Pendyrus and the Treorchy male choirs.

A local all-male choir singing onstage.

The Welsh are especially fond of singing hymns, a tradition that goes back to the days of the Methodist chapels. Their favorites are "Cwm Rhondda" and "Land of Our Fathers," the national anthem. You will hear them sung in schools, at political meetings, at rugby matches, and just about any other place where there is a crowd.

William Williams (1717—91), also called Williams Pantycelyn, was the leader of the Methodist revival in Wales and its chief hymn writer. He wrote some 800 hymns, including "Guide Me, O Thou Great Jehovah." Although Williams had a wider public audience, Ann Griffiths (1776—1805) also composed beautiful hymns, which she wrote down on bits of paper and shared with visiting preachers who came to her house.

A harp maker in his workshop.

FOLK MUSIC AND INSTRUMENTS

Welsh folk music is dear to the Welsh. One of the most popular songwriters is Dafydd Iwan, who uses music to convey political messages. Another well-known musician in Wales is Tudur Morgan. He has worked on collaborations to produce songs based on *The Mabinogion*.

Folk musicians use a number of instruments, but for centuries the harp has been the most important among them. In the 19th century the Welsh triple harp (with three rows of strings) superseded the simple harp. Although once thought to have been invented in Wales, the triple harp was in fact one of the Italian Baroque instruments invented 100 years earlier.

During the 19th century, there was a trend toward classical concert music, which introduced the large, chromatic pedal harp to Welsh music. But the gypsy musicians kept playing the triple harp because it was lighter for them to carry around. Today the triple harp is regarded as the national instrument of Wales. It is used in conjunction with folksinging or as a solo instrument. The most influential triple harpist today is Robin Huw Bowen, who has performed throughout Europe and North America.

One of the most intriguing sites in Cardigan Bay, northern Wales, is an Italian-style village called Portmeirion, conceived by Sir Clough Williams-Ellis (1883—1978). It was a fulfillment of his childhood dream to build a village "of my own fancy on a chosen site."

The village was built gradually over the years from 1925 to 1972 and combines color-washed buildings, statues, and fountains with a variety of architectural styles including Georgian, Victorian, oriental, and gothic. There are about 50 buildings centered on a piazza. These include the luxurious Portmeirion Hotel, which boasts furniture from Rajasthan, India; quaint village cottages; and a shop selling flowered pottery. Portmeirion has been a location for several films and television programs, including the 1960s television series The Prisoner.

ARCHITECTURE

Welsh buildings tend to be simpler than those in England because after the union in 1536, the Welsh aristocrats moved to London, taking the most talented architects and artists with them. Although Wales is not an architectural gem, it does have more castles per square mile than any other country in Europe. There are hundreds of them ranging from Roman fortresses to Norman and Saxon forts. Some of the most impressive are those built by King Edward I.

Some of Wales's most impressive castles are less than 150 years old. These so-called folly castles were built during the 19th century to display the wealth of the nouveau riche, the coal barons and business tycoons who profited from the industrial boom. One of these is Castell Coch, situated just outside Cardiff.

This fairy-tale castle is a reconstruction of a 13th-century castle, complete with a drawbridge and murder holes. The interior is a Victorian fantasy with lavish murals, mirrored ceilings, and walls decorated with scenes from Aesop's fables. It was created by the architect William Burges for his wealthy patron, the Marquess of Bute.

Beaumaris Castle is an ingenious fortress that was built on the Isle of Anglesey to protect shipping in the Menai Strait. Caernarfon Castle in northern Wales is probably the most striking medieval castle in Wales. Its sheer scale and commanding presence are testimony to King Edward's intention for it to be a symbol of English dominance. Its colorful stonework and octagonal towers were modeled on Byzantine castles. In 1969 the castle became internationally famous when Prince Charles was invested there as Prince of Wales.

One of the more famous Welsh architects is Sir Percy Edward Thomas (1883—1969). He is well known for being the designer of civic buildings, including the Swansea Guildhall and the campus of the University of Wales in Aberystwyth.

A view of the **UNESCO-listed Beaumaris Castle**, in the main seaside resort of the Isle of Anglesey in Wales.

Until the 19th century, it was a Welsh custom for a young man to carve a wooden spoon and give it to his sweetheart as an indication of his intention to marry her. Once received, the spoons were often hung on the wall as a reminder of the suitor.

The spoon itself was a symbol that the suitor would take care of his loved one. The designs of the spoons had various meanings, and the maker would choose his own personal symbols. Hearts were popular motifs, and a double heart meant the young man and his girl were united. Miniature houses represented building a home together.

Nowadays love spoons have taken on a wider meaning. They are carved to commemorate events other than marriage and are given as gifts on occasions such as birthdays. Most love spoons today are mass-produced, but those who are sentimental can commission a craftsman to personalize their spoons.

ARTS AND CRAFTS

Wales is a flourishing center for crafts, and Welsh craftsmen have always had an eye for making useful items beautiful. Their Celtic ancestors also had an appreciation of beautiful things, and their art was rather abstract. They liked to use swirling and round shapes, which modern craftsmen have preserved in their pottery, jewelry, woodcarving, and sculpture.

With so many sheep, it is no surprise that Wales has a long-standing tradition of craft in wool. Spinning, weaving, and knitting date back to the days when merchants used to take Welsh stockings and socks to the markets of London. Today you can still find cozy hand-knitted sweaters, woven blankets, and tapestry quilts with skillful embroidery.

Visitors enjoying the artworks, as well as a quiet read, in a gallery at the National Museum in Cardiff.

The Welsh landscape has inspired both native and immigrant painters. Although known as the father of British landscape painting, Richard Wilson spent most of his life in London and Italy, and his paintings were mainly of Welsh subjects. Among Wales's most famous painters are Sir Frank Brangwyn, Cedric Morris, Augustus John and his sister Gwen John, Ceri Richards, and Kyffin Williams.

FILM AND THEATER

Famous Welsh actors and actresses include the late Richard Burton, Sir Anthony Hopkins, and Catherine Zeta-Jones. A recent Welsh heartthrob is Ioan Gruffudd, a Welsh-language soap star who became an overnight sensation after his role as the officer who saved Kate Winslet in the film *Titanic*. He is now a successful actor who lives and works in Hollywood. He has starred in blockbusters, including *Black Hawk Down*, *Hornblower*, and *Fantastic Four*, and has played former British prime minister Tony Blair in the film *W*.

Although the center of British theater is London, Wales has its own theater companies that produce their own plays and invite visiting companies. There

ANTHONY HOPKINS (1937-)

Born in 1937 in Port Talbot, south Wales, Philip Anthony Hopkins was the only child of a baker. He joined a community junior drama club at 17, attended the Welsh College of Music and Drama in Cardiff, and went on to win a scholarship to the prestigious Royal Academy of Dramatic Arts in London in 1961. Obtaining a place with the National Theatre after an audition with his idol, Laurence Olivier, Hopkins went on to enjoy immense stage success at the Old Vic Theatre.

His first film role was in the 1968 movie The Lion in Winter, starring as Richard the Lionheart opposite Peter O'Toole and Katharine Hepburn. Since then, he has appeared in some 90 movies. His portrayal of Hannibal Lecter in Silence of the Lambs, in which he depicted an uncanny intelligence and startling tenderness behind sadistic malice, made him the darling of American audiences. With an Academy Award for Best Actor in his pocket for that performance, he went on to star in the 1992 Merchant-Ivory film Howard's End and 1993's Remains of the Day. His recent films include The Human Stain, Bobby, and Beowulf.

He received the title of Commander of the Order of the British Empire from Queen Elizabeth in 1987 and became an American citizen in 2000.

is a small film culture in Wales, but financial constraints have forced the best talent to look for opportunities elsewhere. Filmmaker Chris Monger returned to south Wales in 1994 to make a well-known film about Wales, *The Englishman Who Went Up a Hill and Came Down a Mountain*, starring Hugh Grant. The Welsh director Endaf Emlyn was nominated for an Academy Award in 1994 for *Hedd Wynn*, a film about a poet killed in World War I. Other famous Welsh directors include Peter Greenaway and Richard Marquand, who directed *Star Wars: Episode VI—Return of the Jedi*.

LEISURE

A paraglider taking off from Constitution Hill in Aberystwyth overlooking the gorgeous blue Cardigan Bay.

LEISURE PLAYS AN IMPORTANT PART in the lives of most Welsh people. For many, sports are the main form of entertainment, although many Welsh people enjoy nature and are known for their appreciation of and talent for music.

Wales's premier sporting venue, the Millennium Stadium, opened in Cardiff in 1999. The stadium is used for all of the country's international rugby and soccer matches, as well as many other sporting and leisure events, such as boxing matches and music concerts.

The Millennium Stadium, or Stadiwm y Mileniwm in Welsh, is the national stadium of Wales and home to some of the largest sporting events in the country.

RUGBY

The sport that really excites Welsh people is rugby. Rugby is a ball game similar to American football: Players attempt to carry an oval ball over the opposing team's line, to score a try, and there are huddles, called scrums. Points can also be scored by kicking penalties over the bar of a pair of H-shape goalposts. Welsh rugby fans are devoted, and matches draw huge crowds of fans clad in red scarves and hats, waving the Welsh flag and carrying leeks, a national symbol.

In 1999 Wales hosted the Rugby World Cup, which is one of the most-watched televised events in the world, after the Soccer World Cup and the Olympic Games. Every year Wales also takes part in the Six Nations tournament contested by the six leading rugby-playing nations in Europe: England, Scotland, Ireland, Wales, France, and Italy. Wales most recently won the Six Nations tournament in 2005 and 2008. Wales's best-known rugby clubs are Ospreys, Cardiff Blues, and Llanelli Scarlets. These teams regularly compete in Europe's premier rugby-club competition, the Heineken Cup.

Welsh rugby fans celebrate their team's victory.

Rugby has come to be regarded as the national game of Wales, and many of the players have become legends. Great players over the years include J.P.R. Williams, Gareth Edwards, and Barry John, who helped the Welsh national team dominate international rugby in the 1970s. Top players since the turn of the century include Shane Williams, Ryan Jones, and Gareth Thomas. Shane Williams is Wales's record all-time try scorer, with 51 international tries.

Teenage boys playing an amateur rugby game in Aberystwyth. Besides supporting their national teams, many Welsh also enjoy playing the sport.

OTHER POPULAR SPORTS

Other popular sports in Wales include football (or soccer as it is called in the United States), cricket, and baseball. Both men and women play football, but fewer women and children go to football matches than men. Cricket is played throughout Wales, and the main team is Glamorgan, which competes with some of the best teams in England. Baseball, an American import, is particularly popular in southeastern Wales. One of the newest spectator sports in Wales is ice hockey, played at the National Ice Rink in Cardiff. Wales also has more than 200 golf courses. The two best known are Royal Saint David's in mid-Wales, which is overlooked by Harlech Castle, and Royal Porthcawl, a 107-year-old course in southern Wales.

There is no shortage of talented athletes in Wales. Colin Jackson, Wales's most famous sportsman, won a gold medal in the 361-foot (110-m) hurdles at the 1993 World Championships in Germany and 1999 World Championships in Seville, as well as a silver medal at the 1988 Olympics in Seoul. Wales also has a national team that competes in the Commonwealth Games, and in 2006, Welsh athletes won 214 medals and ranked ninth out of 53 countries. Young, emerging athletes have also garnered gold medals at the 2008 Beijing Olympics (below).

One of the most successful disabled female athletes is Tanni Grey, who set a world record in 1996 in the Elite Ladies' Wheelchair Marathon in London. Throughout her career she won 16 Paralympics medals, including 11 gold medals. She also won six London marathons and is the holder of 30 world records. She announced her retirement in 2007 and now works as a sports presenter for S4C, BBC Wales, and other broadcasters.

The Sports Council is a government-financed agency that strives to increase participation in sports and to elevate the standards of performance. It provides grants and services to clubs for training and competition. The most talented athletes receive assistance through a program known as Elite Cymru.

CLUBS

Welsh people attach great importance to personal contacts; therefore pubs, clubs, and activity centers play an important part in their lives. In these places they can meet others who share similar interests.

The YMCA, the Scouts, the Girl Guides, and church groups are all active in Wales. The Youth Service in Wales is an organization that aims to develop social and cultural education for young people. Another organization that offers children and young people an opportunity to socialize in Welsh through a range of activities is Urdd Gobaith Cymru. Wales is also one of Britain's largest centers for gymnastics, with more than 60 clubs.

Multisports and leisure centers sprung up in the 1970s and 1980s to cater to the health and fitness craze. The David Lloyd Health and Fitness Club in Cardiff has aerobics classes, a big swimming pool, and a weight-training room.

Women enjoying a dance aerobics class in the Haverfordwest Sports Centre of Pembrokeshire.

Children canoeing on Llangorse Lake in mid-Wales.

BACK TO NATURE

The Welsh are great nature lovers and have a deep respect for the countryside. National parks were set up in the 1950s to conserve Areas of Outstanding Natural Beauty. These national parks offer activities such as hiking, farm holidays, pony trekking, climbing, and canoeing. There are also nature trails and country parks such as the National Watersports Centre at Caernarfon. At the foot of Mount Snowdon, the villages of Beddgelert, Betws-y-Coed, and Llanberis are popular bases for walkers.

BRECON BEACONS NATIONAL PARK

Brecon Beacons National Park is a mix of varied terrain and mountains: In the east lie the Black Mountains; in the west the remote Black Mountain; and throughout are the Beacons themselves, with Pen y Fan, at 2,907 feet (886 m) tall, the highest point in southern Wales. The southern mountains are more challenging than they look, and inexperienced walkers often overestimate how far they can walk. The grass is knee-high in parts, which can slow down walkers, and the mountains look similar, so unless one is a good map reader, it is easy to get lost. The weather there is volatile and harsh. There can be intense rain, heavy mist, and biting winds, not to mention that the temperature drops about 9°F (5°C) for every 3,281 feet (1,000 m) climbed. The Ystrad Felte Falls in the west of the park are even more dangerous. Here ravines, gorges, and fast-falling waters have caused many accidents. That said, for those who are careful, a walk in the park can be a safe yet exhilarating experience.

VACATIONS

Many Welsh like to escape to the seaside. This has been a popular destination for more than 100 years, when seaside resort towns first sprang up to cater to tourists. One of the largest resorts in Wales is Llandudno, where Victorian houses line the shores like those on a picture postcard. Farther south at Porthcawl, campgrounds are dotted along the coast. Here, children can enjoy donkey rides and other amusements.

Another traditional vacation destination is the holiday camp, where accommodation, meals, and entertainment are organized for visitors. These were very popular in the 1950s and 1960s, and Butlins and Pontin's, the companies that manage them, are well-known names. This tradition has declined slightly in popularity during the past 30 years as more Welsh vacation abroad.

Hikers enjoying the view at the Brecon Beacons National Park. .

FESTIVALS

Stilt artists dressed as lobsters at the
Abergavenny Food Festival in Monmouthshire.

I N WALES YOU WILL FIND A FESTIVAL to suit every taste. There are music, art, poetry, literary, dance, and even agricultural festivals throughout the country. Some of these events, such as the National Eisteddfod of Wales, are grand-scale events that draw a large international audience every year.

The Hay Festival of Literature and the Arts, which takes place every spring, is a well-loved and popular festival that attracts book lovers from all over.

The Welsh enjoy the same holidays as the rest of Great Britain, but they also have their own festivals to celebrate their unique culture, music, and language.

People relaxing on the grass in the summer sunshine at the Hay Festival of Literature and the Arts.

The trademark pink pavilions mark the annual National Eisteddfod of Wales.

THE NATIONAL EISTEDDFOD OF WALES

The National Eisteddfod of Wales is the great cultural event in Wales, and it takes place solely in the Welsh language. An *eisteddfod* is simply a public meeting where contests in poetry, music, and literature take place. Hundreds of them are held throughout the year in Wales, but the National Eisteddfod of Wales is world renowned. It dates back more than 100 years and has grown to include everything from poetry to dancing to rock bands. Every competitor dreams of winning the crown or the bardic chair, two of the most prestigious prizes for the best poems. The custom of awarding a chair rather than a trophy goes back to the time when the court poets of a particular king or prince won an official seat, or chair, in the royal household.

The Gorsedd of the Bards awards these coveted prizes with great pomp and ceremony. The Gorsedd is an association of people, or bards, with an interest in Welsh literature and music. A person may become a bard only by being elected by other members and passing an examination in the Welsh language. It was established by an eccentric scholar named Edward Williams (or Iolo Morganwg in Welsh) in 1792. He believed that he was a descendent of an ancient order of druids. Although they have nothing to do with druids, members of the Gorsedd of the Bards are still known as druids and wear different colored robes to signify their rank.

In addition to the National Eisteddfod of Wales, there is the International Musical Festival, held every summer in the small town of Llangollen in northern Wales. Performers from more than 40 countries come here to sing, dance, and play their musical instruments. The festival was established in 1947, and in 1987 the prestigious Choir of the World competition was introduced. In 2005 Luciano Pavarotti honored the festival by adding his name to the competition

The National Museum of Wales is located in Cardiff and includes the National History Museum. Here one can find out more about the history of Wales and see examples of Welsh material culture, such as rural buildings.

"IS THERE PEACE?"

Many of the ceremonies at the National Eisteddfod of Wales are set by the Gorsedd of the Bards. The Eisteddfod alternates between northern and southern Wales. According to tradition, the Gorsedd of the Bards must announce the intention to hold the event one year and a day in advance. The proclamation ceremony takes place around the Gorsedd of the Bards' Circle of Stones, a massive circle of stones assembled according to a traditional plan. A trumpet sounds to call the people together, and once assembled, they chant the Gorsedd prayer. The archdruid performs a ritual of withdrawing the Grand Sword from its sheath three times and crying in Welsh, "Is there peace?" ("Oes heddwch?") to which those assembled reply, "Peace" ("Heddwch.") This ritual is also performed at the crowning, the awarding of the prose medal, and the chairing ceremonies of the National Eisteddfod of Wales.

to demonstrate the influence the festival had on his career. The Urdd National Eisteddfod is a festival for people under the age of 25 that takes place in May.

The largest arts festival in Wales is the Swansea Festival of Music and Arts, held in September or October, which includes theater, opera, dance, jazz, and literary events. Equally important is the Brecon Jazz Festival in August, a three-day festival held in the tranquil town of Brecon.

Another festival is Remembrance Day, which commemorates those who died in World Wars I and II. On and before Remembrance Sunday, which falls on the closest Sunday to Armistice Day on November 11, the Welsh give money to charities and wear poppies.

Schoolchildren performing the floral dance in front of the Gorsedd of the Bards. The Maid of Honor, attended by page boys, is seen holding a horn of plenty.

SAINT DAVID'S DAY

The national day of Wales is Saint David's Day, which is celebrated on March 1. Many people wear leeks or daffodils on this day. Born in the sixth century A.D., Saint David studied for the priesthood, was called to missionary life, and founded numerous monasteries. His burial place, at Saint David's Cathedral in the town of Saint David, is now a center of pilgrimage.

There are many legends about the patron saint of Wales. It is said that when he and his monks first arrived in Glyn Rhosyn, a local chief named Boia was terrorizing the area. To drive out the monks, Boia's wife tried to tempt them to break their vows by sending her maids naked to the monastery. Determined to set a good example, Saint David promptly sent the girls home. It is also said that when Saint David died, a host of singing angels took him to heaven.

There is a famous Welsh saying about leeks: "Wear the leek in your cap, and wear it in your heart." According to legend Saint David told told the Welsh soldiers to wear leeks in their helmets so they could distinguish themselves from the enemy in battle.

CHRISTMAS AND NEW YEAR'S DAY

Christmas and New Year's Day are celebrated in Wales, as in other places around the world, with lots of parties, concerts, and special food.

Christmas celebrates the birth of Jesus and has been celebrated on December 25 since about A.D. 300. Christmas is an important time for Christians. Special church services are held at midnight on Christmas Eve or early on Christmas morning, and Christians celebrate the birth of Jesus by singing hymns and carols. Another tradition in Welsh churches is Christingle, the practice of carrying oranges with lighted candles in them. The orange symbolizes the world, and the candle symbolizes Jesus, the light of the world.

WELSH FOLK COSTUME

On Saint David's Day and other special occasions, you may see Welsh women and children wearing colorful costumes with tall black hats and red cloaks. This is the Welsh national costume, and it developed from the clothing that countrywomen wore in the 19th century—a flannel bathrobe worn as a coat over a striped flannel petticoat with an apron, a shawl, and a cotton cap.

Although there were various styles of dress, Lady Llanover, the wife of an ironmaster in Gwent, was partly responsible for the birth of a national costume. She encouraged people to wear the national dress as a way of instilling national pride at a time when the Welsh felt their identity was threatened.

The idea of a national costume was further reinforced by the work of artists who, in 1840, produced colorful prints of country costumes for the tourist trade. These prints were later developed into postcards depicting Welsh customs and costumes.

In Wales Christmas is called Y Nadolig. In some parts of the country it is the custom to rise early on Christmas morning to attend a church service, called *plygain* (PLUG-eye-n), which means "daybreak" and starts anytime between 3 and 6 A.M. *Plygain* is anything from a short morning service during which carols are sung by visiting soloists to a service lasting until 9 A.M. with as many as 15 carols. The service is often followed by a day of feasting. A standard Christmas dinner consists of stuffed turkey, roast potatoes, and vegetables. In some places toasted bread and cheese, called Welsh rarebit, is washed down with ale. Most people spend Christmas with their families and welcome in New Year's Day with their friends. New Year's Day (Dydd Calan) is the traditional day for presents in Wales. As in many other parts of the world, in Wales the new year is seen as a fresh start and a break from the past. People often try to finish off any business from the previous year and make New Year's resolutions.

More than 4,000 people of all ages dressed as Santa Claus for the annual charity Santa Fun Run in Newtown, Powys.

EASTER

Easter is another Christian festival, this one coming in the beginning of spring. It is a time for families, feasting, and Easter eggs. The egg is an ancient symbol of reawakening that was adopted by the Christians to represent the Resurrection. In northern Wales and Anglesey, children used to go around the neighborhood collecting eggs, rattling clappers (generally used for scaring birds), and chanting rhymes as they made their rounds. Once collected, the eggs were painted and hidden outdoors for an egg hunt. Such age-old customs are far less common now that chocolate Easter eggs have been added to the Easter festivities.

Good Friday, or Gwener y Groglith, is a solemn day when Christians remember the Crucifixion of Christ. Many churches hold services that are stripped of flowers and other adornments, and the church bells are silent.

Hot cross buns are eaten to commemorate the Crucifixion of Christ. The Welsh believe that bread baked on Good Friday will never get moldy because a kind woman gave a loaf of bread to Jesus on the day he was crucified.

Easter Sunday is a very important day to Christians because it commemorates the day that Christ was believed to have been resurrected from the dead. Celebrated on the first Sunday after the full moon following the spring equinox on March 21, Easter Sunday is cheerful, with flowers and church bells. Before sunrise on the joyous Easter Monday, or Llun y Pasg, crowds climb to the highest point in the area to watch the sun "dance" as it rises to honor the Resurrection. In Llangollen, in the Vale of Clwyd, villagers used to greet the arrival of the sun's rays on the top of Dinas Bran with three somersaults. A basin of water was also carried to catch the reflection of the sun "dancing."

New Year's Day (Dydd Calan), January 1

Saint David's Day, March 1

Good Friday (Gwener y Groglith), movable feast

Easter Monday (Llun y Pasg), movable feast

May Day Bank Holiday (Gwyl Banc Calan Mai), first Monday in May

Spring Bank Holiday (Gwyl Banc y Gwanwyn), last Monday in May

Summer Bank Holiday (Gwyl Banc yr Haf), last Monday in August

Remembrance Sunday, closest Sunday to November 11

Christmas Day (Dydd Nadolig), December 25

Boxing Day (Gwyl San Steffan), December 26

Morris dancers bring back this 15th-century traditional dance during the May Day celebrations.

MAY DAY BANK HOLIDAY

The first Monday of May is traditionally a holiday to celebrate spring's arrival. In the past everyone collected green branches to decorate their houses and danced around a maypole presided over by a May Queen. There are still May Day celebrations in many parts of Wales, such as Cardiff, where the celebration includes maypole dancing, music, clowns, carnivals, food, and drink.

Britain owes its bank holidays to Sir John Lubbock, a member of Parliament and, not surprisingly, a banker. Lubbock believed that there should be more statutory vacations to ease the burdens of the working class. In 1871 he managed to pass the Bank Holidays Act in Parliament. This forced all banks to close on the first Monday in May, and because there were no banking facilities, other employers had to close on that day as well. Additional legislation followed, giving Britain more bank holidays. Most Welsh like to take a short break at the seaside during these occasions.

HALLOWEEN

An example of a festival that is not a public holiday is Halloween, on October 31. Associated with the supernatural, it is celebrated with bonfires, candles, and sometimes fireworks. Children dress up as witches and ghosts and go around the neighborhood asking for candy. A popular game is apple bobbing. Apples are placed in a large bowl of water on the floor. Children then try to pick up an apple only with their teeth. Another custom is for a young man to walk around the churchyard a few times at night wearing his coat and vest inside out and reciting the Lord's Prayer backward. This courageous youth then puts his finger through the keyhole of the church door to prevent any spirits from escaping. It was once believed that the apparitions of those who would soon die could be spied through the keyhole. In more-rural areas, young men dress up in sheepskins and old ragged clothes and blacken their faces. After chanting weird rhymes, they are given gifts of apples, nuts, or beer.

A group of Aberystwyth University students in costume as zombies and witches on Halloween night.

FOOD

A bartender serves up a pint of his popular beer.

AUNIQUE WELSH BREAKFAST includes local eggs and bacon served with laverbread, which is made from seaweed, and cockles. Afternoon tea is usually served with a fruit bread called *bara brith* (BAR-ah breeth) or Welsh cakes, which are simple little drop scones.

The traditional meat for dinner in the evening is Welsh lamb. A popular snack could be Welsh rarebit, a dish made with a savory sauce of melted cheese and served over hot toasted bread.

A popular, well-stocked local delicatessen in Cardiff.

Welsh cooking is simple and wholesome. Milk, butter, cheese, and oats are common to many recipes, as is lamb. Traditional cooking techniques include roasting, simmering, and baking on a griddle. There are many tasty dishes such as roasted lamb with herbs, savory pies, hearty stews, cakes, and steamed puddings.

Locals catching a quick bite at a food joint in Monmouthshire.

MEALS

Meals can be confusing in Wales. The types of food, the time it is eaten, and what the meal is called vary throughout the country. The description below is a generalization.

Most Welsh people start the day with a light breakfast of tea and toast or cold grain. When it is cold outside, they might eat hot oatmeal, a favorite in many parts of Great Britain. Some people might have a cup of tea or coffee, and a cookie or a piece of cake around 11 A.M. On the weekend they might have a traditional fry-up. This is a full breakfast of fried eggs, bacon, sausages, bread, and perhaps tomato, which is washed down with lots of tea.

Lunch is usually eaten at around 1 P.M. If it is a main meal, it may be called dinner. But in the cities it is more common for people to eat a quick sandwich at lunch and their main meal at 6 or 7 P.M. Depending on which part of Wales you are in, this may be called dinner, supper, or tea. The meal might consist of meat, fish, or a stew and is usually eaten with potatoes and a vegetable.

Welsh people do not eat out nearly as often as Americans do, but there are some typical eating places that they frequent. Besides pubs, people might eat in a café during the day. Sometimes called workman's cafés, these offer cheap, filling meals in a relaxed atmosphere. After a long day at work, some people might prefer a quick "takeaway" of fish and chips or Indian or Chinese food. Fast food, including McDonald's and Pizza Hut outlets, has also found its way to Wales.

During the 19th century, drunkenness was a problem in the coal-mining towns. The Methodists frowned upon drinking, but this did not deter the miners. The temperance movement campaigned to ban drinking but only succeeded in doing so on Sundays.

DRINKS

Although there are a few independent breweries and one or two companies making Welsh whiskey, on the whole Wales does not produce much alcohol. The Welsh still drink lots of tea, coffee, and soft drinks but are not exactly teetotalers. The average Welshman enjoys his beer, which is very much the national drink of Wales. Although beer is the most popular alcoholic drink, wine is becoming more commonly drunk throughout Great Britain. Country wines, made from wildflowers and weeds, and ginger beer are also popular in Wales. At Christmas some people drink mead made from fermented Welsh honey and mulled wine, which is a type of spiced wine.

BEER

There is a tradition of brewing beer at home, one that still persists in rural Wales. In the 19th century farmers brewed beer for their workers, who expected beer or cider with their meals. Most social occasions such as weddings, christenings, and even funerals were observed with plenty of beer. In the 19th century brewing became large scale, and the bigger foreign breweries came to south Wales to supply beer to thirsty miners, steelworkers, and dockworkers. The Welsh like English beers and bitters but still prefer their own brews. Brains is Cardiff's locally brewed beer.

The diet of the past was frugal but tasty. Farmers, miners, and factory workers needed nourishing food that could be prepared quickly at the end of the day. In north Wales a popular harvesting snack was a dish called *siot* (SHOT), made by soaking oatcakes in buttermilk. In south Wales a favorite dish at lunchtime was *sucan* (SOOK-an), a cold sour grain soup.

Barrels of local beer can be found in pubs throughout Wales.

The pub (short for "public house") is an institution throughout Great Britain, and Wales is no exception. The pub is an informal place where people can meet, share a drink, and have a chat. In the old days pubs served nothing but beer and spirits, but these days they also serve coffee, tea, and hot food. There are no waiters in a pub, and if you want to eat or drink something, you have to go and get it yourself at the bar.

People go to the pub quite regularly and will often step in for a quick drink after work. The pub owner knows most of his customers personally and often chats with the regulars. In Wales even a stranger can enjoy a conversation with a pub owner. And if he happens to be busy serving customers, there is usually another charming Welsh person with whom you can strike up a conversation!

A typical Welsh cream tea and treats in Carmarthenshire.

FOOD

Typical Welsh cuisine includes dishes such as roast meats, pies, cakes, jams, and puddings. Many of the dishes have simple ingredients. Dairy herds are in abundance in Wales, so it is no surprise that traditional cooking methods use lots of milk, butter, and cheese. The best-known cheese is Caerphilly cheese, which used to be a lunchtime favorite of the miners. Welsh rarebit is a traditional snack eaten throughout Wales. To make it, you pour a mixture of milk, cheese, eggs, and ale over toast.

Lamb features in many recipes. It can be roasted with cider and rosemary, stewed with potatoes and leeks, or cooked with scraps of vegetables in a broth. Lamb and mutton pies are also popular in Wales.

Wales is a fish lover's paradise. Fine salmon and trout are caught in the rivers, and cockles are gathered from the sands along the coastline. Many of the coastal towns used to be busy ports, and there are still good catches of cod, sole, and lobster.

LAVERBREAD

Laverbread (sometimes called Welsh caviar), or *bara lawr* (BAR-ah LOWR), is a delicacy in Wales. It is edible seaweed, or laver, that is processed into a greenish black gelatin. Since the seaweed grows on coastal rocks along the beaches, from which it is harvested by hand, the supply of laverbread tends to be erratic, as heavy swells occasionally cover it in sand so that it cannot be easily gathered. Unprocessed algae is also eaten by North Americans and Northern Europeans, and is known as dulse in Canada and the United States and dillisk in Ireland.

Various types of seafood sold at a store in Wales.

Laverbread is very popular in southern Wales. It is rich in minerals and vitamins and was once eaten by miners who worked underground because it helped to combat vitamin deficiencies stemming from a lack of sunshine and fresh air. Laverbread used to be sold door-to-door by women who carried packets of laver in big baskets. Now it is sold in supermarkets and specialty shops. Laverbread can be served coated with oatmeal and fried with bacon or made into a sauce to accompany fish or mutton.

SWEET SENSATIONS

There are all sorts of pastries and bread in Wales. Currant bread, or *bara brith,* is spicy, speckled fruit bread made from flour, yeast, and currants that have been soaked overnight in tea. Crumbly Welsh cakes are baked on a griddle, served with sugar, and laden with dried fruit and spices. These are teatime favorites that used to be served to tired travelers at inns before supper. Oatcakes and pancakes made with buttermilk are also popular, as are currant buns and bread pudding. Honey, apples, and soft fruits such as berries grow well in the south, and the Welsh know just how to preserve them as jams and jellies to spread on toast or as chutneys for meat.

In some parts of northern Wales, toffee-making parties used to be a traditional part of Christmas and New Year's festivities. A light supper would be followed by games, storytelling, and the making of toffee. The toffee mixture would be boiled and then poured onto a stone slab. The guests would butter their hands, peel off the toffee, and eat it.

Welsh lamb has a delicate flavor developed through slow maturing on natural pastures. On Sundays many families get together to enjoy a hearty meal known as the Sunday lunch. This is a big meal of roast lamb served with potatoes and gravy, followed by a dessert such as apple pie.

WELSH LAMB PIE

1 large pie

1½ pound (680 g) lamb neck

1 small bunch young carrots

1 teaspoon (5 ml) finely
chopped parsley

Pepper and salt

Pie pastry dough

Milk

1 medium onion

- Bone the meat and cut into small pieces.
- Wash and slice carrots into thin rounds.
- Layer carrots in the bottom of a baking dish, followed by meat, parsley, and pepper and salt. Repeat until all is used.
- Cover with water, stopping at 2 inches (5 cm) from the top.
- Roll out the pastry large enough to cover the top of the dish.
- Cut a small hole in the center of the pastry.
- Cover the baking dish with the pastry and brush over with milk.
- Bake for two hours at 350°F (180°C).
- Meanwhile, boil the bones with one onion, pepper, and salt for 1½ hours.
- When the pie is ready, strain the boiled liquid and pour into the pie through the hole on top.
- Serve hot or cold.

BARA BRITH (SPECKLED FRUIT BREAD)

2 loaves

12 ounces (340 g) mixed dried fruit

7 ounces (198 g) soft brown sugar

12 fluid ounces (360 ml) cold tea

7 ounces (198 g) molasses sugar

10 ounces (283 g) unbleached plain flour

2 teaspoons (10 ml) baking powder

1 teaspoon (5 ml) freshly ground mixed spice

1 large egg, well beaten

2 1-pound (454-g) loaf tins, greased and lined

- Soak the fruit and the soft brown sugar in the tea, cover, and let stand overnight.

- The next day stir in the molasses sugar, mixing well.

- Sift the flour, baking powder, and spice together, and mix thoroughly into the fruit mixture.

- Stir in the beaten egg until everything is well mixed. Divide the batter into two loaf tins.

- Bake at 350°F (180°C) for 40—45 minutes.

- To serve, slice and spread thickly with butter

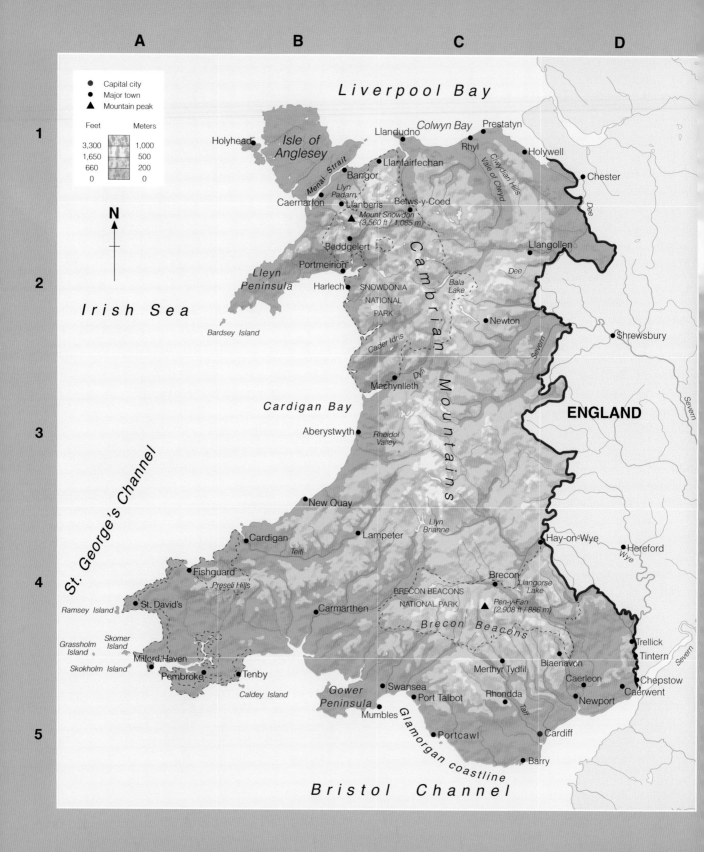

A   **B**   **C**   **D**

Legend:
- ● Capital city
- • Major town
- ▲ Mountain peak

Feet	Meters
3,300	1,000
1,650	500
660	200
0	0

N

1

Liverpool Bay

Holyhead

Isle of Anglesey

Llandudno   *Colwyn Bay*   Prestatyn

Rhyl   Holywell

Chester

Llanfairfechan

Menai Strait

Bangor

Llyn Padarn

Caernarfon   Llanberis   Betws-y-Coed

Vale of Clwyd   *Clwydian Hills*

Dee

▲ Mount Snowdon
(3,560 ft / 1,085 m)

Llangollen

2

Irish Sea

Beddgelert

Portmeirion

Lleyn Peninsula

Harlech

SNOWDONIA NATIONAL PARK

Dee

Bala Lake

Cambrian

Bardsey Island

Cader Idris

Newton

Shrewsbury

Cardigan Bay

Dyfi

Machynlleth

Mountains

Severn

3

Aberystwyth

Rheidol Valley

ENGLAND

Severn

New Quay

Cardigan

Teifi

Lampeter

Llyn Brianne

Hay-on-Wye

Hereford

Wye

4

St. George's Channel

Fishguard

Preseli Hills

Brecon

Llangorse Lake

Ramsey Island

St. David's

Carmarthen

BRECON BEACONS NATIONAL PARK

▲ Pen-y-Fan
(2,908 ft / 886 m)

Trellick

Grassholm Island

Skomer Island

Brecon Beacons

Tintern

Severn

Milford Haven

Skokholm Island

Pembroke

Tenby

Blaenavon

Merthyr Tydfil

Caerleon

Chepstow

Caldey Island

Gower Peninsula

Swansea

Rhondda

Caerwent

Newport

Taff

Mumbles

Port Talbot

Cardiff

5

Portcawl

Barry

Glamorgan coastline

Bristol Channel

MAP OF WALES

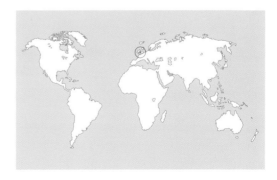

ECONOMIC WALES

Services

 Airport

 Ports

 Tourism

Agriculture

 Dairy

 Sheep

Manufacturing

 Aluminum plants

 Oil refinery

 Steel making

Natural Resources

 Coal

 Limestone

 Slate

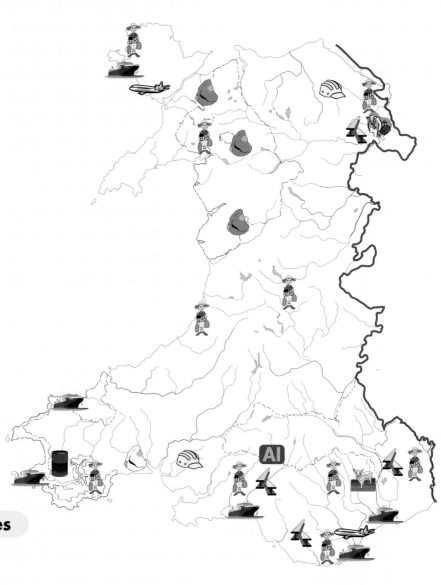

ABOUT THE ECONOMY

OVERVIEW

Since devolution in 1999, the Welsh have felt more responsible and accountable for managing their own economy. Devolution has allowed them to take charge of their own economic affairs, including tackling the current global financial crisis and helping the unemployed get back to work. Today Wales's service industry is the strongest performer, contributing almost two-thirds of the country's gross value added (GVA). Its manufacturing sector accounts for a third of its GVA, and agriculture, forestry, and fishing contribute slightly more than 1 percent. As part of the United Kingdom, Wales uses the pound sterling issued by the Bank of England. In addition to the service industry, sectors such as real estate, public administration, defense, health, and education are important. Tourism is another sector that contributes significantly to the Welsh economy.

REGIONAL GROSS VALUE ADDED (GVA) BY UK REGION

£45,610 million/$70,015 million (2008 estimate)

CURRENCY

$1 = £0.65 (2010 estimate)

REGIONAL GROSS VALUE ADDED (GVA) BY INDUSTRY

Real estate, renting, and business activities: 18.6 percent
Manufacturing: 17.9 percent
Agriculture: 0.4 percent
Construction: 7.1 percent
Wholesale and retail trade: 11.1 percent
Health and social work: 10.1 percent
Public administration/defense: 6.9 percent
Education: 7 percent (2007 estimate)

UNEMPLOYMENT RATE

11 percent for males and 7.2 percent for females (2010 estimate)

AGRICULTURAL PRODUCTS

Grains, oilseed, potatoes, vegetables, cattle, sheep, poultry, fish

INDUSTRIAL PRODUCTS

Machine tools, electric power and automation equipment, communications equipment, metals, chemicals, coal, petroleum, food processing, textiles, clothing, and other consumer goods

MAIN IMPORTS

Manufactured goods, machinery, fuels, foodstuffs

MAIN EXPORTS

Sheet metal, automotive parts, electronics

MAIN TRADE PARTNERS

United States, Germany, Netherlands, France, Ireland, Belgium, Spain, China, Norway, Italy (2008 estimate)

CULTURAL WALES

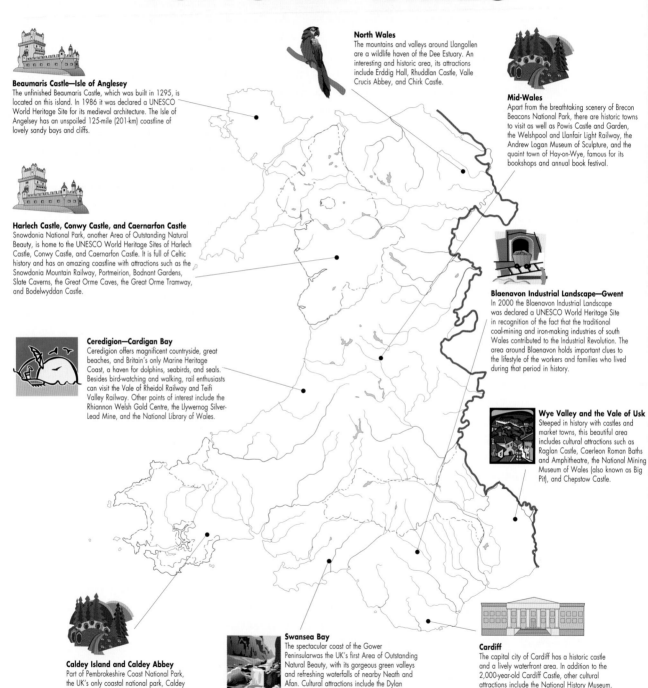

Beaumaris Castle—Isle of Anglesey
The unfinished Beaumaris Castle, which was built in 1295, is located on this island. In 1986 it was declared a UNESCO World Heritage Site for its medieval architecture. The Isle of Angelsey has an unspoiled 125-mile (201-km) coastline of lovely sandy bays and cliffs.

North Wales
The mountains and valleys around Llangollen are a wildlife haven of the Dee Estuary. An interesting and historic area, its attractions include Erddig Hall, Rhuddlan Castle, Valle Crucis Abbey, and Chirk Castle.

Mid-Wales
Apart from the breathtaking scenery of Brecon Beacons National Park, there are historic towns to visit as well as Powis Castle and Garden, the Welshpool and Llanfair Light Railway, the Andrew Logan Museum of Sculpture, and the quaint town of Hay-on-Wye, famous for its bookshops and annual book festival.

Harlech Castle, Conwy Castle, and Caernarfon Castle
Snowdonia National Park, another Area of Outstanding Natural Beauty, is home to the UNESCO World Heritage Sites of Harlech Castle, Conwy Castle, and Caernarfon Castle. It is full of Celtic history and has an amazing coastline with attractions such as the Snowdonia Mountain Railway, Portmeirion, Bodnant Gardens, Slate Caverns, the Great Orme Caves, the Great Orme Tramway, and Bodelwyddan Castle.

Blaenavon Industrial Landscape—Gwent
In 2000 the Blaenavon Industrial Landscape was declared a UNESCO World Heritage Site in recognition of the fact that the traditional coal-mining and iron-making industries of south Wales contributed to the Industrial Revolution. The area around Blaenavon holds important clues to the lifestyle of the workers and families who lived during that period in history.

Ceredigion—Cardigan Bay
Ceredigion offers magnificent countryside, great beaches, and Britain's only Marine Heritage Coast, a haven for dolphins, seabirds, and seals. Besides bird-watching and walking, rail enthusiasts can visit the Vale of Rheidol Railway and Teifi Valley Railway. Other points of interest include the Rhiannon Welsh Gold Centre, the Llywernog Silver-Lead Mine, and the National Library of Wales.

Wye Valley and the Vale of Usk
Steeped in history with castles and market towns, this beautiful area includes cultural attractions such as Raglan Castle, Caerleon Roman Baths and Amphitheatre, the National Mining Museum of Wales (also known as Big Pit), and Chepstow Castle.

Caldey Island and Caldey Abbey
Part of Pembrokeshire Coast National Park, the UK's only coastal national park, Caldey Abbey, home to Cistercian monks, is located on tiny Caldey Island off the coast of Tenby.

Swansea Bay
The spectacular coast of the Gower Peninsularwas the UK's first Area of Outstanding Natural Beauty, with its gorgeous green valleys and refreshing waterfalls of nearby Neath and Afan. Cultural attractions include the Dylan Thomas Centre, the Swansea Maritime and Industrial Museum, and Swansea Museum.

Cardiff
The capital city of Cardiff has a historic castle and a lively waterfront area. In addition to the 2,000-year-old Cardiff Castle, other cultural attractions include the National History Museum, the fairy-tale Castell Coch, and the Millennium Stadium and Millennium Centre.

OFFICIAL NAME
Principality of Wales

CAPITAL
Cardiff

POPULATION
About 3 million (2009 estimate)

OFFICIAL LANGUAGES
Welsh, English

AREA
8,108 square miles (21,000 square km)

WELSH NATIONAL EMBLEMS
The leek, a vegetable with a cylindrical bulb and leaves, and the daffodil, a plant with yellow flowers and a trumpetlike corona

CLIMATE
Maritime climate. Rainfall is frequent; annual average: 55 inches (1,397 mm). Annual mean temperature: 50°F (10°C)

HIGHEST POINT
Mount Snowdon (3,560 feet/1,085 m)

NATIONAL PARKS
Snowdonia, Pembrokeshire Coast, and Brecon Beacons

AREAS OF OUTSTANDING NATURAL BEAUTY
Gower Peninsula, Lleyn Peninsula, Isle of Anglesey, Clwydian Range, Wye Valley

MAJOR LAKES
Bala, Llangorse

MAJOR RIVERS
Dee, Severn, Wye

ISLANDS
Anglesey, Bardsey, Caldey, Grassholm, Ramsey, Skokholm, Skomer

COUNTIES
Clwyd, Dyfed, Gwent, Powys, Gwynedd, Mid Glamorgan, South Glamorgan, West Glamorgan

MAJOR RELIGION
Christianity, primarily Protestant including Nonconformist. Roman Catholicism is a growing minority.

IMPORTANT HOLIDAY
Saint David's Day (March 1), a holiday to commemorate the patron saint of Wales

IMPORTANT CULTURAL EVENT
National Eisteddfod of Wales

TIME LINE

IN WALES	IN THE WORLD

A.D. 50–55
The Romans begin their conquest of Wales.

407
The last Romans leave Wales and Britain.

855–6
Rhodri the Great becomes king of Powys
and defeats the Vikings.

1170
Owain Gwynedd, ruler of north Wales, dies.

1240
Llywelyn ab Iorwerth the Great, monarch of
Wales, dies.

1255
Llywelyn ap Gruffydd becomes prince of
Gwynedd.

1267
Henry III recognizes Llywelyn ap Gruffydd
as Prince of Wales.

1277
King Edward of England invades Wales, aided
by Llywelyn ap Gruffydd's brother and Prince
Gruffudd ap Gwenwynwyn of Powys.

1282–3
The English finally conquer Wales.

1294–5
The Welsh rebel but are defeated.

1301
Edward of Caernarfon, later King Edward
II, becomes the first English Prince of Wales.

1400
Owain Glyndwr leads the warriors of
Gwynedd in a bloody revolt against the English.

1404
Owain Glyndwr captures the castles at
Aberystwyth and Harlech and convenes a
parliament in Machynlleth.

1413–5
Owain Glyndwr's rebellion comes
to an end.

1534
Henry VIII declares himself head of the
Church in England and Wales.

1536
The Acts of Union unite Wales with England.

1206–1368
Genghis Khan unifies the Mongols and starts
conquest of the world. At its height, the Mongol
Empire under Kublai Khan stretches from China
to Persia and parts of Europe and Russia.

IN WALES	IN THE WORLD

1642
Civil war begins between King Charles I and Parliament, with Wales showing loyalty to the king.

1648
The Royalist rebellion is defeated.

1649
The Prince of Wales becomes King Charles II.

1707
Scotland is united with England and Wales to form Great Britain.

1820
King George III of England dies and is succeeded by his son George IV.

1916–22
David Lloyd George of Wales serves as the prime minister of Britain.

1924
A Welsh nationalist party is formed.

1969
Britain's Prince Charles is invested as the Prince of Wales.

1999
The first-ever general election to choose the Welsh National Assembly is held. The Labour Party captures 28 of the 60 seats while the nationalists take 17 seats. A purpose-built chamber is due to be erected nearby. Pressure grows on Alun Michael to deliver match-funding for the Objective One European aid package for Wales, worth about £1.5 billion ($2.3 billion). As the issue drags on, Plaid Cymru threatens a vote of no confidence in his leadership.

2000
The Welsh National Assembly debates the no-confidence motion, and Alun Micm,hael resigns as first secretary before the vote is carried. He is replaced temporarily by Rhodri Morgan.

2002
Newport is declared a city.

2008
The European Union formally recognizes Welsh language as a minority tongue.

1776
U.S. Declaration of Independence

1789–99
The French Revolution

1914
World War I begins.

1939
World War II begins.

1997
Hong Kong is returned to China.

2001
Terrorists crash planes into New York, Washington D.C., and Pennsylvania.

2003
War in Iraq begins.

GLOSSARY

bara brith (BAR-ah breeth)
Currant bread.

bara lawr (BAR-ah lah-war)
Laverbread, also called Welsh caviar. It is edible seaweed processed into a greenish black gelatin.

bard
Celtic singer or the winner of a competition at an *eisteddfod*.

Celt
Gaul or member of Celtic-speaking peoples.

coracle
A small, oval rowing boat made of skins or tarred or oiled canvas stretched on a wicker frame.

Cymru
"Wales" in Welsh.

druid
A priest among the ancient Celts of Great Britain, Gaul, and Germany, or an *eisteddfod* official.

eisteddfod (ACE-deth-vord)
A competitive congress of Welsh bards and musicians.

gorsedd (GOR-seth)
A meeting of bards and druids.

gwyniad
A whitefish found in Bala Lake.

Industrial Revolution
The social and economic changes resulting from the mechanization of industry that began in England about 1760.

The Mabinogion
A Welsh manuscript of the 14th century.

Neolithic
Characteristic of the last phase of the Stone Age, from 9,000 to 8,000 B.C.

Nonconformist
A Protestant separated from the Church of England

plygain (PLIG-in)
A church service early on the morning of Christmas

pub
Common term for a public house, which is an inn or a tavern

S4C
Sianel Pedwar Cymru, or Channel Four Wales

Welsh rarebit
Welsh dish of toasted bread and a mixture of cheese, eggs, milk, and ale

FOR FURTHER INFORMATION

BOOKS

Atkinson, David and Neal Wilson. *Wales* (Lonely Planet Country Guide). 3rd rev. ed. Oakland, CA: Lonely Planet Publications, 2007.

Davies, John. *A History of Wales.* Rev. ed. New York: Penguin, 2007.

Deary, Terry. *Wales* (Horrible Histories). New York: Scholastic, 2008.

Evans, Gwynfor. *Land of My Fathers: 2,000 Years of Welsh History.* Talybont, Wales: Y Lolfa, 2008.

Jenkons, Simon. *Wales: Churches, Houses, Castles.* London: Allen Lane, 2008.

Le Nevez, Catherine, Paul Whitfield, and Mike Parker. *The Rough Guide to Wales.* 6th ed. London: Rough Guides, 2009.

Winn, Christopher. *I Never Knew That About Wales*. 3rd. ed. London: Ebury Press, 2007.

FILMS

Magic Islands and Harbours—Wales at Its Magnificent Best. Go Entertain, 2006.

Visions of Wales (Travel Aerial Photography). Delta Visual Entertainment, 2008.

Visit Wales with Rachel Hicks. Camrose Media, 2008.

Wales—A Nationhood. Pegasus Entertainment, 2005.

Wales—A Walk Through the Countryside. Fastforward, 2006.

Welsh Journeys with Jamie Owen. Go Entertain, 2006.

MUSIC

Treorchy Male Choir. *Great Voices of Wales: Sons of Rhondda.* Music, 2006.

Various Artists. *The Best of Wales.* EMI, 2005.

Various Artists. *Land of My Fathers: The Best of Welsh Male Voice Choirs.* Performance, 2006.

BIBLIOGRAPHY

BOOKS

Boyes, Vivien. *The Druid's Head.* Llandysul, Wales: Gomer Press/Pont Books, 1997.

Ifans, Rhiannon. *The Magic of the Mabinogion.* Talybont, Wales: Y Lolfa, 1993.

Jones, Mairwen and John Spink. *Are You Talking to Me?* Llandysul, Wales: Gomer Press/Pont Books, 1994.

Lowson, Nigel. *A New Geography of Wales. Cambridge,* England: Cambridge University Press, 1991.

Sheppard-Jones, Elisabeth. *Stories from Welsh History.* Ruthin, Wales: John Jones Publishing, 1998.

Thomas, Dylan. *A Child's Christmas in Wales.* London: Orion Publishing Group, 1986.

WEBSITES

All-Biz.info: State Wales, www.uk.all-biz.info/regions/?fuseaction=adm_oda.showSection&rgn_id=3&sc_id=7

BBC News: Profile—Wales, http://news.bbc.co.uk/1/hi/world/europe/country_profiles/6233450.stm

BBC: Wales Society and Culture, www.bbc.co.uk/wales/culture/sites/aboutwales/pages/culture.shtml

Castles of Wales, www.castlewales.com/

Central Intelligence Agency: World Factbook—United Kingdom, www.cia.gov/library/publications/the-world-factbook/geos/uk.html

Facts about Wales, www.facts-about.org.uk/places-geography-wales.htm

Gwybodiadur.co.uk: the Welsh-Language Media, http://gwybodiadur.tripod.com/media.htm#newsmag

Intute: World Guide—Wales, www.intute.ac.uk/worldguide/html/1071.html

Office for National Statistics: Wales—Its People, www.statistics.gov.uk/CCI/nugget.asp?ID=452

Visit Wales, www.visitwales.co.uk

Wales Index, www.walesindex.co.uk

Wales.com, www.wales.com

Walesdirectory.co.uk, www.walesdirectory.co.uk/tourists.htm

Welsh Assembly Government, www.wales.gov.uk

Welsh Assembly Government: Statistics, www.statswales.wales.gov.uk/TableViewer/tableView.aspx?ReportId=4916

Welsh Books Council, www.wbc.org.uk

Welsh Icons, www.welshicons.org.uk/html/famous_welsh.php

INDEX

INDEX